CLINICAL DIRECTORATES IN THE IRISH HEALTH SERVICE

About the Author

Yvonne O'Shea, RGN, RM, RNT, B.A. Public Administration (Health), MSc. Econ. (Policy Studies), Ph.D., was the first clinical directorate nurse manager in Ireland. She spent a number of years at St James's Hospital, Dublin, first as nurse tutor and subsequently as assistant director of nursing and nurse manager in the CResT clinical directorate. She was involved in the introduction of the clinical directorate model in St James's and conducted detailed research into clinical directorates as part of her role. She was nurse manager of the multidisciplinary team responsible for the successful bid to establish a new cardiac surgery unit in St James's Hospital and co-author of the successful tender document.

Yvonne O'Shea is currently chief executive of the National Council for the Professional Development of Nursing and Midwifery. During her time as chief executive, the National Council has been responsible for the development of a comprehensive clinical career pathway for nurses and midwives that has resulted in the creation of over 2,000 clinical nurse specialist/clinical midwife specialist posts, and 120 advanced nurse practitioner/advanced nurse practitioner posts. In addition, over 20,000 nurses and midwives have participated in additional professional development opportunities provided by the National Council. In cooperation with An Bord Altranais, the National Council has been instrumental in introducing the prescribing of medications by nurses and midwives.

Her career has included experience in general nursing, midwifery, nurse education, nurse management, nurse regulation and professional development. Prior to joining the National Council, she was chief education officer at An Bord Altranais, where her achievements included the *Review of Scope of Practice for Nursing and Midwifery* and the introduction of the *Framework for the Scope of Nursing and Midwifery Practice*. She is the author of *Nursing and Midwifery in Ireland: A Strategy for Professional Development in a Changing Health Service* (Blackhall Publishing, 2008).

CLINICAL DIRECTORATES IN THE IRISH HEALTH SERVICE

Managing Resources and Patient Safety

Yvonne O'Shea

BLACKHALL
Publishing

This book was typeset and published by

Blackhall Publishing
Lonsdale House
Avoca Avenue
Blackrock
Co. Dublin
Ireland

e-mail: info@blackhallpublishing.com
www.blackhallpublishing.com

A catalogue record for this book is available from the British Library.

Printed in Ireland by Colour Books Ltd

*To my colleagues, the staff of the National Council and
to all present and past members of the National Council,
in recognition of the contribution they have made through
their work over the last ten years, to improved health care
services for patients.*

CONTENTS

Contents

LIST OF FIGURES

LIST OF TABLES

LIST OF ABBREVIATIONS

A&E	Accident & Emergency
ABI	acquired brain injury
AMP	advanced midwife practitioner
ANP	advanced nurse practitioner
BAMM	British Association of Medical Managers
BMA	British Medical Association
CEO	chief executive officer
CIM	clinicians in management
CIS	clinical information system
CME	centre for midwifery education
CMG	clinical management group
CMHT	community mental health team
CMM	clinical midwife manager
CMO	chief medical officer
CMS	clinical midwife specialist
CMT	clinical management team
CNE	centre for nurse education
CNM	clinical nurse manager
CNS	clinical nurse specialist
COPD	chronic obstructive pulmonary disease
CResT	cardiology, respiratory and cardio-thoracic surgery (clinical directorate at St James's Hospital, Dublin)
CT	CAT scan (computerised axial tomography)
DHSS	Department of Health and Social Security (UK)
DNS	director of nursing services
DOHC	Department of Health and Children
DRG	diagnosis related group
EAGs	external advisory groups
EBP	evidence-based practice
ECRI	Emergency Care Research Institute
EMG	executive management group
ERG	external reference group
EU	European Union
EWTD	European Working Time Directive
FETAC	Further Education and Training Awards Council

FOI	Freedom of Information (Act)
FSAI	Food Safety Authority of Ireland
GP	general practitioner
HIQA	Health Information and Quality Authority
HIS	hospital information systems
HIT	health information technology
HR	human resources
HSE	Health Service Executive
HSRP	health service reform programme
HTA	health technology assessment
ICP	integrated care pathway
ICT	information and communication technology
ICU	intensive care unit
IHSM	Institute of Health Services Management
IMB	Irish Medicines Board
IMS	information and management services
INO	Irish Nurses Organisation
IT	information technology
IV	intravenous
MedEL	medicine for the elderly (clinical directorate at St James's Hospital, Dublin)
METR	medical education, training and research (HSE)
MHC	Mental Health Commission
MHID	mental health of intellectual disability
MRI	magnetic resonance imaging
National Council	National Council for the Professional Development of Nursing and Midwifery
NCVA	National Council for Vocational Awards
NHO	National Hospitals Office (HSE)
NHS	National Health Service (UK)
NMPDU	nursing and midwifery planning and development unit
NSF	national service framework
NZGG	New Zealand Guidelines Group
OHM	Office for Health Management
OPM	Office for Public Management
OTC	Office of Tobacco Control
ORIAN	operating rooms, general intensive care unit, high dependency unit, day surgery unit, laser unit, endovascular unit, sterile supplies unit and

	anaesthetics (clinical directorate at St James's Hospital, Dublin)
PAM	professionals allied to medicine
PAS	patient administrative system
PCCC	primary, community and continuing care (HSE)
PCT	primary care team
PHN	public health nurse
R&D	research and development
RCA	root cause analysis
RCN	Royal College of Nursing
RCN	registered children's nurse
RGN	registered general nurse
RM	registered midwife
RM	resource management
RMHN	registered mental health nurse
RMI	Resource Management Initiative
RNID	registered nurse intellectual disability
RNP	registered nurse prescriber
SDO	service delivery and organisation (national R&D programme (NHS))
SEA	specify, enable and assure (HSE quality and clinical care directorate)
SIMT	serious incident management team
SKILL	Securing Knowledge Intra Lifelong Learning
SSI	Social Services Inspectorate
TD	Teachta Dála
UK	United Kingdom
US	United States
WHO	World Health Organisation

FOREWORD

The reform of the health services in Ireland has been a major policy priority of the Government for the last ten years. The objective of this policy is to provide a health service that is of a high quality and places the safety and welfare of patients at the centre. Health care policy also aims to ensure that the resources that are allocated to the delivery of the health services are used in the most efficient and effective manner possible. Involving clinicians in the management of health services and in determining the best use of resources has been shown to support the achievement of these policy objectives.

The clinical directorate model for the management of health services is based on the principles of partnership and integration. It requires cultural change, such as devolution of power and responsibility. Clinical involvement in management and reform is one of the most powerful forces for quality patient care improvement.

Dr O'Shea examines the implications of the clinical directorate model for the role of nurses and midwives in the management and delivery of health services and provides a resource of information, analysis and reflection.

Nursing and midwifery occupy a central role in the provision of health services in Ireland. The clinical directorate model represents moving from professional silos towards integrated multidisciplinary teams, putting the patient at the centre of our health care and creating a culture of professional collegiality.

Mary Harney, TD
Minister for Health and Children

FOREWORD

Clinical directorates are central to the HSE's commitment to having clinicians function as senior clinical leaders and decision-makers in the public health service. The decision to implement the clinical directorate model on a nationwide basis was a major milestone in the health service transformation programme of the HSE, which represented the intended culmination of the Health Service Reform Programme that began in 2003. With the introduction of clinical directorate structures, we have, for the first time, the prospect of significantly empowering clinicians as the key designers and leaders of modern health services at all levels right across the organisation.

We know from experience that when care services have significant leadership from clinicians they deliver far better results in terms of clinical effectiveness, patient safety, patient outcomes and financial returns. The implementation of clinical directorates, the creation of a national Quality and Clinical Care Directorate within the HSE and the merging locally of our hospital- and community-based services creates a unique opportunity and momentum to achieve this. Health services from around the world have expressed interest in the approach being adopted by the HSE and we now have the potential to create a model that would facilitate the delivery of high quality and sustainable health care.

This book represents a timely contribution to the process of health care reform in Ireland. It emphasises the importance of involving clinicians in management as a new approach built on a foundation of trust and co-dependency between clinicians and managers. This book emphasises the importance of using the clinical directorate structure to drive and accelerate change and to ensure that the links within and between acute and community care services are strengthened and focused on simplifying patient journeys and care pathways.

Dr Barry White
National Director of Quality and Clinical Care, HSE

INTRODUCTION

The motivation for writing this book comes from two sources. The first of these stems from the role of the author as chief executive of the National Council for the Professional Development of Nursing and Midwifery. Since its foundation in 1999, the National Council has provided leadership to the professions of nursing and midwifery in the development and enrichment of their role within the Irish health services. This has resulted in the development of clinical career pathways in response to service needs for the professions, from general nurse or midwife to specialist and advanced practice. The introduction in Ireland in 2008 of the clinical directorate model as the accepted method for the organisation of health services and the involvement of clinicians in the management of these services is one of the most significant developments to happen in the Irish health services in recent years. It poses major changes for all clinical professions. The interest of this author is principally in the challenges it poses for nurses and midwives and the opportunities it presents to them of enhancing their contribution to high quality, safe, patient-centred care, in partnership with other clinical professionals.

The second motivation for writing this book stems from the fact that, in 2008, the author wrote a book entitled *Nursing and Midwifery in Ireland: A Strategy for Professional Development in a Changing Health Service*.[1] This book was based on extensive qualitative research conducted with 115 senior health service professionals, both clinical and non-clinical. It set out to map the future role for nursing and midwifery within a health service that was undergoing enormous change. The book was published before it became clear that the clinical directorate model was to provide the basis for the new contract for medical consultants and was destined to revolutionise the way in which health services were to be managed in Ireland for decades to come. This development presented a challenge to complete the work started in the first book by examining its implications for the role of nurses and midwives in the management and delivery of health services. There has also been a significant deterioration in the state of the national finances in the intervening period, which has made the question of resource management within the health services in Ireland all the more challenging. There is considerable pressure on all forms of public expenditure and on health care expenditure in particular. The need for new approaches to resource management, therefore, is particularly relevant now.

This new book provides an opportunity to explore the history and evolution of clinical directorates over the last thirty years in order to arrive at a deep understanding of the thinking behind them and the impact they are likely to have on Irish health services. It also provides Irish clinical professionals with a resource to assist them in understanding the clinical directorate model and their own role within it.

The book is about making the right choices in the management of health services. It suggests that the involvement of clinicians in management, and in making decisions about how resources are used, in acute and primary settings, is the most efficient way to guarantee the effective use of resources and the safety of patients. The term 'clinician' refers to a medical professional who works directly with patients. This includes consultant and non-consultant doctors and general practitioners, working in hospitals and in the community. It also includes nurses and midwives working as general, specialist or advanced practice nurses or midwives, in acute and primary care settings. The term also refers to other health and social care professionals, such as social workers, physio-therapists, occupational therapists, dieticians and others.

Clinical professionals in modern health care settings rarely work in isolation. They are increasingly organised in multidisciplinary teams usually, although not exclusively, headed by a doctor. Clinical directorates represent a particular structure for this kind of multidisciplinary teamwork. The clinical directorate model is being introduced into the Irish health service system with the premise that medical consultants will provide clinical and executive leadership to multidisciplinary teams of clinical professionals, each one responsible for making his or her specific contribution to patient care and safety.

Clinical directorates represent an approach to the management of health services that is now quite common in the health care systems of many developed economies. It is based on the involvement of clinicians in making decisions about the choices involved in how resources should be used. Health services are expensive. They consume large amounts of public expenditure. In 2009, the Health Service Executive (HSE) budget amounted to €14.7 billion and the HSE had close on 130,000 employees. Decisions about how best to use these resources can make the difference between life and death for individual clients of the health services. The use of clinical directorates, as a model of management and decision-making, is based on the premise that those who make decisions about the use of the resources that are available should include those who possess the knowledge about how resources can be used to best effect. The involvement of clinicians, therefore, is essential to optimise the use of resources and to ensure the greatest possible level of safety in patient care. The introduction of clinical directorates as a way of managing health services represents a new culture that involves managers and clinicians cooperating to build a more efficient fit-for-purpose health service.

Those who have management responsibilities within the health service are called on to make many choices every day. These choices give rise to questions such as:

- What is the most appropriate setting for the delivery of health care for an individual client or patient?
- What is the best mix of skills and competencies necessary to ensure that each patient or client receives the care they need?
- How much money should we spend on technology and/or drugs for the delivery of health care?

Decisions about these choices, and thousands like them, affect each day the lives of patients and clients of the health services and determine the way in which vast amounts of public money are spent. They also affect the quality and safety of care that patients and clients receive. In that sense, therefore, this book is about patient safety. Those who are responsible for the delivery of clinical care are held accountable for the way in which they perform their duty. They are accountable for patient safety. The clinical directorate approach is based on the premise that those who are to be held accountable for the delivery of effective and safe health care should be involved in making decisions about how the resources that are available for that purpose are allocated.

The book is divided into eight chapters. Chapter 1 explores how the involvement of clinicians in management in the United Kingdom (UK) emerged principally from a concern about the management of resources. Chapter 2 traces developments from an earlier period in the United States (US) back to the UK and how the National Health Service (NHS) adapted the model of clinical directorates to its own cultural and economic realities. Chapter 3 traces early developments in the creation of clinical directorate experiments in the UK and in Ireland and includes original research material from the time, based on interviews with front-line participants involved in the change management process. Much of the research behind this book is based on original research conducted by the author in 1994 and 1995 while working on the introduction of clinical directorate structures within St James's.

The introduction of clinical directorates in Ireland is an integral part of the most recent programme of reform of health services in Ireland. Chapter 4 reviews the key moments in the design and implementation of this reform strategy and provides the policy development context in which recent developments in the implementation of clinical directorates should be understood. The momentum for continued reform of the health services received an enormous boost with the publication of *Building a Culture of Patient Safety*, the Report of the Commission on Patient Safety and Quality Assurance, in 2008.[2] Chapter 5 examines the recommendations of the Commission's report and the importance of patient safety as a key principle that should drive the development and implementation of structures designed to ensure that clinical accountability is reflected in management and institutional arrangements. The Commission recommended that the clinical directorate structure should be used as a vehicle for ensuring the involvement of clinicians in the management of services. The report makes it clear that the key to patient safety is clinical governance based on accountability across multidisciplinary clinical teams in which each team member takes responsibility for their own specific contribution to the patient's journey and care pathway.

Chapter 6 examines the most recent developments leading up to the establishment of clinical directorates throughout the whole of the health services in Ireland. Chapter 7 places the development and introduction of clinical directorates in Ireland within the context of the emergence of an integrated approach to governance, quality assurance and risk management within the HSE. It also examines the core concept of clinical leadership on which the movement towards increased involvement of clinicians in management is based. This chapter also examines the institutional arrangements that have been developed within the HSE to support the clinical directorates and the development of clinical leadership throughout the system.

Chapter 8 addresses the principal motivation behind the idea for this book by examining the implications for nurses and midwives of the introduction of clinical directorates. It sets out to identify the issues that clinical directorates raise for nursing and midwifery and to take stock of relevant recent developments within the professions. It also seeks to identify the impact that the introduction of clinical directorates will have on the professions in the care settings in which they operate and to list the principal implications and make recommendations regarding the involvement of the professions in the development and implementation of clinical directorates and integrated services.

The conclusion reflects on the challenges and opportunities that the introduction of clinical directorates presents to all clinical professionals and health service managers in Ireland and the lessons learned over the thirty years during which clinical directorates have developed and evolved.

Yvonne O'Shea

CHAPTER 1

The Resource Management Initiative in the UK

Origins

In a modern health service, management cannot be the sole concern of managers. A model of management in which managers focus solely on the most efficient use of resources, while clinicians concentrate only on providing the best care for their patients, is an inbuilt prescription for conflicts of interest at every turn. Similarly, a model in which clinicians are concerned only with their patients, while administrators take responsibility for the health of the community as a whole, is no more workable. The aims of national, regional and local administrators and clinicians must be brought into harmony, partnership and shared goals. And this, since professional managers, in practical terms, cannot acquire the skills of clinicians, can only be achieved by clinicians taking on a management role and responsibility. Clinicians will do so only if the proper commitment, structures and resources are in place, and if it is to the benefit of their patients, careers and professions. This much is now obvious but it was not always so and it took the health services in the UK and Ireland, with some notable exceptions, a long time to arrive at this conclusion and to take the necessary action to make it a reality.

The introduction of the clinical directorate concept into the Irish health service was influenced by the UK experience. At the end of the Second World War, the British Labour Party, following its general election victory, established the National Health Service (NHS) in 1948 as one of the principal pillars of the welfare state proposed by the British economist and social reformer William Beveridge in what became known as the *Beveridge Report*.[3] Up until then, patients were, by and large, required to pay for their health care. Under the NHS, services would henceforth be provided by the same doctors and the same hospitals, but were provided free at the point of use; services were financed from central taxation and everyone was eligible for care.[4]

The introduction of the NHS was widely welcomed but encountered initial opposition from the medical profession. To overcome this, the Government accepted key demands from the doctors. The principle of clinical freedom was formally recognised. For specialists, there was a part- or whole-time salary plus merit awards, and the right to treat private patients in NHS hospitals. For general practitioners (GPs), there was a capitation system that was as far removed from a salary as possible. Like it or not, the state and the medical profession had become mutually dependent.

In subsequent years, the Government pursued the objective of stretching scarce resources in the administration of the NHS by improving the quality of management. Up until the 1980s, the NHS was administered rather than managed. It had a 'command and control' system of planning, with delivery of services effected through a range of statutory regulations, guidance documents, operating instructions and delegated freedom. The largest share of resources was devoted to meeting the pressures on the acute hospital sector.[5] The NHS found itself under constant and increasing pressure to not only reduce costs in relative terms, but also, at the same time, provide new and expanded services.

It became evident that there was an inherent conflict between the demands of professional management and the clinical freedom exercised by clinicians. As one commentator noted at the time:

> Clinical freedom created a political dimension outside any normal managerial framework. As quickly as efficient management reduced long-established queues, medical science opened new ones. Clinical freedom allowed consultants to make decisions affecting resources, and consultants had to be persuaded if they were to make their clinical demands more modest. A long and divisive conflict was in prospect.[6]

The emergence of clinical directors with responsibility for the quality of their services was an eventual outcome of the Griffiths Inquiry Report into NHS management, published in 1983,[7] which found that the NHS had no coherent system of management at a local level, a situation it summarised in its much-quoted observation, 'if Florence Nightingale were carrying her lamp through the corridors of the NHS today she would almost certainly be searching for the people in charge'. Griffiths concluded that clinicians should be involved more closely in management decisions and should have a fully developed management budget and the necessary administrative support. This was designed to prompt some measurement of output in terms of patient care.

As it happened, the first use of a clinical directorate model in the UK, at Guy's Hospital in London (see Chapter 2), occurred within a year of the publication of the Griffiths Report. It would be some time before the model was generally accepted in the UK, but the general thrust of the approach was given considerable impetus by Griffiths. Underpinning the recommendations of the report was a rejection of the 'consensus' style of management and the introduction of general managers in health authorities, hospitals and units with the aim of strengthening strategic management and accountability by putting in place structures for line management and devolved budgets. Griffiths argued that doctors' decisions largely dictated the use of all resources and it was therefore necessary to involve the clinicians more closely in the management process, consistent with clinical freedom for clinical practice. Clinicians should participate fully in decisions about priorities in the use of resources and should accept the management responsibility that goes with clinical freedom. This implied active involvement in securing the most effective use and management of all resources.

The Griffiths Inquiry recognised that a crucial element in the introduction of general management was the need to find a way of involving doctors, and senior doctors in particular, in the day-to-day management of the NHS. During the 1980s, various models were tried. None was successful until the model of the clinical directorate pioneered by Guy's attracted interest and support.

On foot of the Griffiths Inquiry's recommendations, a Management Budgeting experiment was organised in 1983 in four acute and two community sites and was extended in 1985 to fourteen acute sites. Under Management Budgeting, budgets were devolved to smaller units, supported by improved information, and with clinician collaboration. It was predominantly finance-led and a top-down strategy, with no real linkage to clinical practice. It was not a success. Medical staff were not committed, they felt no ownership of the project and viewed it with distrust. Nurses in particular felt left out. Management Budgeting also suffered from the fact that, for the most part, information systems within the participating sites were under-developed. In 1986, a review of Management Budgeting[8] concluded that it had failed to achieve its principal objectives and a new approach was necessary. But one significant benefit came from Management Budgeting: it prepared the way for the Resource Management Initiative (RMI).

RMI was the first systematic attempt in the UK to involve doctors as a group in the management process. It was an acknowledgement that the management and flow of resources within the NHS could not be managed effectively without doctors individually determining the allocation of resources through their decisions about patients. Professor Peter Spurgeon[9] noted that RMI had one big drawback in the limitations of information technologies at the time: information systems were not sufficiently advanced to provide essential financial and activity data to track and assess allocation decisions. The initiative also had the problem of seeking to involve clinicians in a process that was concerned with restraining the use of resources rather than having a primary focus on the care patients received. Although RMI was ultimately regarded as unsuccessful, many lessons were learned that are worthy of analysis.

The Resource Management Initiative

In 1986, the Department of Health and Social Security (DHSS) formally announced a national experiment in six acute hospitals that became known as the Resource Management Initiative.[10] The DHSS launched the initiative as a new approach to resource management and the experiment would show whether or not this approach would result in measurable improvements in patient care. The aim of RMI was to enable the NHS to give a better service to patients by helping clinicians and other managers to make better informed judgements about how the resources they controlled could be used to maximum effect. RMI had two main components: (1) a management structure that explicitly gave clinicians responsibility for budgets and integrated them into the hospital decision-making process, and (2) the development of an information system for monitoring the cost-effectiveness of services.

The six sites chosen were Arrowe Park Hospital, Wirral Health Authority; Freeman Hospital, Newcastle; Guy's Hospital, Lewisham and North Southwark Health Authority; the Royal Hampshire County Hospital, Winchester; Huddersfield Royal Infirmary; and Pilgrim Hospital, South Lincolnshire. These sites varied in size and location and represented a balance between teaching and non-teaching establishments. They were intended as pilot sites capable of acting as reference sites for the rest of the NHS.

One of RMI's distinguishing characteristics was the involvement of clinicians and nurses from the beginning. The six pilot sites were chosen largely on the basis of the existing involvement of doctors and nurses in management. The sites also represented different levels of experiences in previous initiatives, such as the failed Management Budgeting experiment. Freeman and Huddersfield were second-generation Management Budgeting sites. Having entered the experiment much later in the process, Guy's had been involved with earlier clinical budgeting experiments. Freeman and Guy's had assisted in the Griffiths Inquiry. Guy's and Royal Hampshire had already adopted strong sub-unit organisational structures based on the clinical directorate model. All six were at different stages of development of information systems.

Subsidiary objectives of RMI included providing information for clinicians that would enable them to:

- Identify areas of waste and inefficiency
- Benefit from clinical group discussion and review
- Highlight areas that could benefit from more resources
- Identify and expose the health care consequences of given financial policies and constraints
- Understand the comparative costs of future health care options and hold informed debates about such options

The DHSS also set criteria that could be used to determine whether the implementation of RMI would be successful or not. These criteria were framed in the form of questions that each hospital management team needed to answer. These were:

- Has the management scheme fully involved the clinicians?
- Has this enabled the clinicians to have a positive influence on the management of resources of the hospital?
- Have the information systems provided data relevant to patient care and has the information been of value to clinicians in providing that care?
- What have been the direct and indirect costs of implementing the scheme and have these costs been justified by the resulting benefits of the scheme?
- Has the time input required by clinicians to implement the scheme been considered by the clinicians themselves to be beneficial to patient care?

The Brunel Evaluation

The DHSS commissioned the health economics research group at Brunel University to undertake an external evaluation of the costs and benefits of RMI. The group issued an interim report, *Resource Management: Process and Progress*,[11] in 1989, which reported that resource management (RM) was not to be found across the whole hospital in any of the six sites and that there was more of an expectation of benefits in the future from the changes that had been introduced than any hard evidence of benefits up to that point.

The Brunel Group defined RM as a cycle involving the following stages:

- Service providers collaborate in setting objectives, priorities and plans
- Resources are allocated to service providers to achieve agreed priorities
- Service providers exercise responsibility for managing the resources they commit
- Service provision and resource use are regularly monitored
- The value of the service provided is reviewed

RM, it said, must involve the service providers who demand and use resources in the decision-making process about how and where these resources are allocated. Doctors, nurses, paramedical staff and managers of support services must be included in the process. This approach had implications for the roles of management within the hospital, whether they were senior executives with overall responsibility for the hospital or functional managers with divisional or departmental responsibility. Their role changed from one of direction to one of facilitation and monitoring.

For RM to work, service providers needed access to information about resource use and related activity. It was important that this information was relevant, accurate and timely. Service providers would consequently spend more time analysing and interpreting data. Similarly, the service providers required authority and accountability and a new management structure was necessary to ensure this. The RM sites that focused on changing the management structures stated that a sub-unit structure like clinical directorates was essential to the implementation of RM. The Brunel team suggested that the RM process was required simultaneously at different levels in the hospital:

- **Level 1** was where a clinical firm or ward applied the process. Commitment by key individuals, such as consultants and ward sisters, to take on a proactive role in managing resources was critical. There was a need for devolved budgetary authority if individuals were to take responsibility for managing resources.
- **Level 2** was where a clinical directorate applied the RM process. Decisions made by senior hospital management outside the directorate would, of course, affect the ability of the personnel within the directorate to make decisions; similarly, within the directorate, individual service providers would be affected by the decisions of their colleagues. Collaboration and consensus was essential, both within the directorate (between disciplines) and between the directorate and corporate management. Management was increasingly less about direction than consensus. Any change in activity would affect all disciplines in resource use. Information supply and support specialist skills were important in helping the sub-units to manage resources.
- **Level 3** was where the hospital as a whole was involved in RM. In such cases, senior management must be willing to devolve authority. It was a totally decentralised model of hospital management.

The Brunel team argued that effective resource management, therefore, was primarily about involving those responsible for committing resources in the management process and, secondly, about having a comprehensive, accurate and timely information system. Fundamental to success was the involvement of doctors in the management of the hospital. Investment to produce integrated hospital information systems, with features such as ward ordering of tests, drugs and supplies, resulted in added benefits in terms of operational effectiveness and enhanced the range of inputs into the case-mix database. In short, RM project management involved changing management culture and creating usable information.

An NHS review, *Working for Patients*,[12] published in 1989, reinforced the RM trend by emphasising the importance of doctors being involved in management, sub-unit organisations with a focus on specialty groupings, medical audits and the provision of activity and cost information. This review made proposals for NHS trusts, or self-governing hospitals, and this dominated public discussion at the time and somewhat distracted from the RM movement. The

Government also introduced the GP contract, performance related pay and a patients' charter. It is possible that the introduction of the contract system, whereby purchaser health authorities contracted for the delivery of health care from provider hospitals, may have distorted the RM model. Nonetheless, the NHS review announced that RM had become approved policy and would be rolled out across the NHS.

Evaluation Findings

The Brunel team reached some important conclusions in its interim evaluation. The team believed that the major achievement of the experiment to date was that RM had been adopted mainly at sub-unit level in most sites, involving a general move towards sub-unit organisational structures. RM represented an enormous change, particularly in relation to the culture of the organisation and the need to invest in information technology (IT).

In general, the team found that computer systems were incomplete; the focus had been on in-patient data activity and the resources they used, with some work beginning on outpatients. Case-mix costing was not well developed and, where it existed, it was still very crude. Work on outcome measurement was very patchy and was still mainly at research stage. The quality of data improved over time, reflecting the commitment of consultants to the coding process. But progress was very uneven over the sites. Training was insufficient; it was not planned for at any of the sites and, in general, the situation did not improve as the project progressed. RM for nurses was implemented separately and there was a tendency for nursing issues to be marginalised in the whole process.

The Brunel team recognised that implementing RM was a highly complex task involving the simultaneous development of information systems, change management and day-to-day management of the organisation. The scale of organisation development was initially underestimated in terms of the cultural revolution it implied and the impact on individuals and structures; some attempts to remedy this were made at some of the sites as the project progressed. However there was an overall lack of planning and foresight.

A project manager and team in each site carried out project planning and project management. The team was made up of hospital staff, district staff and representatives of companies involved in designing and implementing computer systems. The composition of both the project teams and the steering committee varied, with the hospital general manager, director of nursing services and consultants generally on both. They focused on the implementation of new computer systems and the organisation and delivery of training courses. Each site had a steering committee with links to the DHSS. The evaluation noted that project planning was frequently weakened by the absence of clearly articulated information strategies. This was often further exacerbated by the fact that project managers lacked the authority and support to implement the required changes.

The Brunel team concluded that the costs of introducing RM were difficult to define. It was difficult to separate costs that were attributed to it from those that were attributable to non-RM activities. The estimates of additional expenditure on RM, excluding hospital information systems (HIS) development, in the period 1986/1987 to 1989/1990 ranged from £354,000 to £2.6 million. These were more than double the top-of-the-range costs expected by the DHSS. It was calculated that total investment costs represented an additional cost per in-patient episode of between £7.80 and £27.30, an increase of between 1.4 and 3.3 per cent. If HIS costs were included, costs would increase to 11.3 per cent per patient episode. These figures would need to be increased by 20 to 45 per cent if the opportunity cost of reallocated staff time were included.

The team found very little clear evidence of benefits from RM. Managers welcomed and emphasised the cultural change. Doctors were now directly involved in management and discussions were able to take place on the basis of improved information. There were no measurable improvements in patient care, though there were some perceptions of improvement. Responses to a survey of consultants in the directorates of medicine and general surgery at the six sites suggested that only 21 per cent said that RM had improved patient care, with 49 per cent saying that it would in the future improve patient care. Forty-one per cent of nurses stated that RM had improved patient care, with 76 per cent suggesting it would do so.

Key Issues

An overall analysis of the six sites, based on the interim Brunel report, highlights a number of key issues on which there was either a divergent approach or a convergence of practice. These issues can be summarised in three key areas: organisation and structure, information systems and the management of change.

Organisation and Structure

The sites had to determine the most appropriate structure to ensure the involvement of service providers in the management of the hospital and, in particular, whether a traditional or a clinical directorate structure was the most appropriate. The related modifications necessary for operational success also had to be determined and, where appropriate, implemented. There was no standard RM organisation pattern that was seen as an inevitable component of the initiative. The Royal Hampshire and Guy's hospitals maintained that their organisation and structure made implementation of RM possible, having moved to a directorate structure prior to being involved in the RM initiative. Other sites, such as Freeman and Huddersfield, saw organisation as more flexible and maintained that it could be adapted to the needs of RM as it developed.

The traditional model in hospitals had been for consultants to relate individually to general managers. Medical committees elected a small executive group to exercise some collective responsibility for medical performance and activity. Functional managers held budgets. The hospital management executive consisted of medical representatives, the director of nursing, and senior managers responsible for specific functions such as finance, personnel and support services. Freeman, Huddersfield and Pilgrim hospitals favoured this traditional model with modifications. Its application to RM suggested the need for 'dual drive' planning and programming by both hospital managers, according to their views of hospital priorities and increased knowledge of activities, and individual clinicians, according to their increased knowledge of the implication of their activities. This might result in increased medical representation on the management executive. Service providers needed assistance with information collection and interpretation. This might result in business managers and nurse managers being attached to clinical groupings, even though clinicians were not similarly involved.

Guy's Hospital pioneered the directorate model in the UK. The Royal Hampshire and Arrowe Park also adopted this structure. The Freeman went some way towards directorates by the introduction of clinical heads of specialty departments, with the Pilgrim testing the idea in some specialities. The directorates had a head: the clinical director, who was managerially accountable for the operational work of all staff within the directorate, except for consultant staff, because of clinical freedom and collegial assumption. A nurse manager and a business manager provided managerial assistance. The nurse managers were accountable for the operational management of the directorate of nursing services and the nursing budget. Business managers could work full-time in a directorate or be required to work between two. They acted as managerial assistants and advisers to the clinical directors. They were concerned with information collection and interpretation. They also provided an important bridge with general management in the wider hospital. Arrowe Park operated a variant of the model, with one managerial role in each directorate, accountable to the clinical director and accountable for the work of non-clinical staff within the directorate. The hospital operated a policy of positive discrimination in appointing nurses to these posts, which combined the nurse and business manager roles. Clinical directors were members of the hospital management executive.

The clinical directorate model raised a number of operational issues, such as, what were the right boundaries for a directorate? And, should paramedical functions be included within the structure? Guy's created new management structures below directorate level, with some of the directorates being subdivided into clinical groups. The paramedical and other support service functions may not have been included within directorates but were managed by heads of departments and accountable to the chief executive. The sites considered a number of possibilities to include the services within the directorate structure: make them either singly or in combination directorates in their own right; or attach them to the closest 'natural host' among the clinical directorates that sell their services to other directorates. Both of these possibilities preserved the cohesion of the functions, with the latter running the risk of creating inequalities in provision between directorates. A third possibility was to divide the functions between the directorates so that each directorate has its own pharmacist, physiotherapist, etc. This may have been a more equitable solution but ran the risk of fragmenting functions and weakening professional career patterns.

There was a need to create new processes for planning resource allocation, management, monitoring and service review. The clinical director had to create mechanisms for working with the nurse and business manager. In the sites, the directorates developed a pattern of weekly meetings. The clinical director also needed to find a mechanism to work with consultant colleagues; monthly meetings were held in the directorates across the sites.

Chief executives and general managers were required to devolve much of their former decision-making to the directorates, yet they remained accountable for ensuring that services were delivered in accordance with policy and within budgetary limits. The hospital management executive became a forum for clarifying and debating between formulated priorities rather than itself creating the priorities. The role of hospital managers evolved increasingly towards that of supporting and facilitating rather than directing services. Consideration had to be given to how much administrative support was required by providers to meet their responsibilities. Sites experimented with different combinations of business and nurse managers at specialty or directorate level.

Information Systems
It should be borne in mind that information technology was then in its infancy in 1989. Both computer technology and software development were, by today's standards, primitive. In evaluating RMI, it was found that there was a convergence in the basic pattern of information systems development. In general, operational systems fed into a case-mix database. The Royal Hampshire implemented an integrated operational system, with a network of terminals in wards and departments that had a single interface with the case-mix database. In the other sites, feeder systems sent data separately to case-mix. Some sites developed electronic links between feeders and case-mix, while others adopted tape and disk transfer. The nature of the information available from the computer systems generally included operational information (used in the day-to-day running of the hospital), management information (for use in planning, monitoring and reviewing at hospital, specialty/ directorate and ward level) and professional information (enabling service providers to monitor and review their own work).

Five of the six sites had nursing IT systems that varied greatly in the data they collected. In most instances, off-the-shelf packages were used, which required a lot of modification. Some systems were based on stand-alone personal computers and were used for managing wards. Other systems were linked to the case-mix system, where aggregated data was used for managing groups of wards. There was little convergence in approach to the design of nursing systems, and, in general, many of these systems were subsequently to be dropped altogether or significantly reduced in terms of their applications.

Sites had to put a lot of effort into ensuring accurate and complete data. Coding was consequently moved closer to the clinician. Emphasis was placed on achieving good activity data rather than on refining costing data. Collection of data on the outcomes of in-patient treatment was patchy across most of the sites. The approach to defining information needs and the relative success of the approaches adopted varied greatly. Report generation facilities from the case-mix database were in the process of being designed. The five sites with case-mix systems were all experimenting with the diagnosis related group (DRG) classification system. The hospitals that had a directorate structure were less advanced in implementing the case-mix system. Both Guy's and the Royal Hampshire had used financial and activity information for planning and monitoring at both hospital and directorate level prior to the introduction of the case-mix system.

Service providers needed support in handling and manipulating data from the system to facilitate decision-making. In some sites, business managers were being trained in the use of the case-mix system and other computer packages and were the principal handlers for the directorate. At other sites, individuals were being trained to interrogate the database on behalf of service providers. All sites with the case-mix system in place had a central team for maintenance.

Management of Change

Local 'champions' who occupied key positions, such as clinicians, general managers and nurse managers, were crucial in starting and continuing the RM momentum. The implementation of RM and the programme of change it entailed required substantial manpower capacity within the hospitals. It was important to allocate responsibility for the process to individuals who could take day-to-day responsibility for implementing RM. Just as important, ownership of the problems and the solutions needed to be retained within the hospitals. The role of the project manager in coordinating the implementation of RM was critical, and this was particularly true where external consultants were used to assist in implementing RM.

Old and new systems had to be maintained. The change in management structure and information systems needed to be managed in parallel. There was a need for support, which included keeping staff informed through meetings, seminars, open days and newsletters; and training, especially in the use of information systems and dealing with problems such as the flow of junior doctors. Induction training was needed for new nurses through the use of temporary trainers, who were usually service providers seconded to implement the new systems and organisation development, to ensure that RM became an integral part of the process of management and service delivery.

Different sites had different emphases. For example, the Freeman Hospital put a lot of emphasis on information systems initially, while organisational and managerial change drove the pace of change in the other sites, such as Guy's. However, it should be noted that if developments on either of these two areas became too far out of step, frustration and tensions arose. People concerned with change issues in the six sites were asked to describe the main issues to be resolved in the RM initiative and the key triggers for change. Six issues and seven key triggers for change were identified.

The six issues were:

- **Defining and understanding RM and RMI**: Being clear about what RM was and where it was going.
- **Values and power**: Who decided what and how? What were the boundaries between practitioners, patients, managers and politicians?
- **Skill mix needs**: It was unlikely that there were many clinicians or managers immediately capable of carrying out the complete management role.
- **Exploiting information**: How to make information decision-led and not data-led, and clinical-practice-led rather than finance/computer specialist-led.
- **Intervention and maintenance processes, not merely structure**: Structure was important. Processes (systems and communications) needed for daily routine activities of the hospital, clinical feedback, management routines, quality assurance, etc. needed to be effective and user-friendly.
- **Designer cultures**: There was a need to strike a balance between management roles, job design, processes and structures.

The seven triggers for change were:

- **Crisis/emotion**: Based on a strong feeling of the need for change even prior to the RM initiative because of problems and crises being experienced.
- **Unit computing**: Based on a strong desire to secure independent hospital information capacity.
- **Systems and information knowledge**: Based on a gradual acquiring of knowledge by key personnel in the hospital, enabling them to influence the direction of policy and events.
- **Using new information**: New insight into what was happening was a strong force for change.
- **Product champions**: People seized with a vision and the ability to make it happen.
- **Role of clinical heads**: Perhaps the most critical trigger for change and very much related to the organisation structure that was put in place to enable the role to develop.
- **External issues** with the health services, including political issues.

Exploiting information and the intervention processes were highly important issues that needed to be resolved to trigger change. Sorting out the role of clinical heads and acquiring the capacity to use and fully exploit new generations of information were of the essence.

Lessons Learned

The Brunel team published a final report on its evaluation of the RM initiative[13] in April 1991. This confirmed the general thrust of the interim findings. It noted that, in launching the initiative, there had been unrealistic optimism about timescales and costs. This may have contributed, in part, to a loss of momentum when participants began to realise that the objectives set for the initiative were taking longer than anticipated to realise. The real resources required extended beyond financial support: shortages of key skills within the service and a lack of relevant experience in some suppliers contributed to a slower pace of progress. Four years on, the team said that it was still assessing implementation at the sites, rather than being able to review a period of post-implementation established use and, on the balance of evidence, it was not yet possible to provide a definitive assessment of RM as an ongoing working process for hospital management.

However, the Brunel team were, in many respects, positive about the value of the RM processes and structures. At each of the sites, there had been substantial progress towards full implementation. None had abandoned the project. On the contrary, key managers said that they did not want to go back to previous ways. Elements of the RM process had taken root at all sites, with service providers demonstrating a greater level of proactive management. Moreover, there was a strong logic to resource management. The team believed that RM resolved the problem of enabling service activities to be managed effectively rather than management being divided between resource allocation and patient care – an NHS problem of long standing. They saw RM as a means of promoting collaboration amongst service providers, and between service providers and management. In this way, authority and decision-making accountability regarding the allocation and management of resources and the planning and review of services were integrated into a coherent whole.

The team's evaluations were subsequently published as a book: *Hospitals in Transition: The Resource Management Experiment.*[14] The team summarised resource management as a process that brought service providers and general management together to collaborate in determining how best to commit available resources, strategically and operationally, based on their knowledge of the requirements and implications of delivering patient treatment and care. The most important characteristics demonstrated by the six pilot sites were the willingness to collaborate across professional boundaries, and the alignment of authority and accountability for the allocation of resources.

The authors observed that, in moving from the traditional model of hospital management to the RM model, control moved downward, from the unit to the sub-unit and closer to service delivery. The sub-unit was now the hub of the hospital, and the task of the unit was to coordinate and integrate the activities of the sub-units, as well as activities that were also taking place between the sub-units. In this model, collaboration became paramount, because it was effective only if those at sub-group level were prepared to work to common objectives.

Among their conclusions, the authors made the significant point that resource management was evolutionary and open-ended; there would be no end point. Ultimately, there was no boundary between implementation of RM and the organisation that was transformed as a result. This meant that implementation was as much a part of RM as the process: so *how* it was implemented determined whether or not the organisation could be transformed. It was not possible to implement poorly yet end up with a satisfactory process.

Because the Brunel team carried out its assessment in the implementation phase, there are a number of important lessons to be learned from the analysis of the resource management initiative for those who are about to embark on, or are in the early implementation of, any initiatives where resource planning involving clinician participation is a core factor:

- RM was, first and foremost, about cultural change. Involving service providers in planning and managing resources had implications for all groups within the organisation. Information technology was subsidiary to this. If the cultural change aspect of the project was not properly managed, RM would not succeed. This required total commitment from the senior management within the hospital.
- If RM was to work, it had to become part of the management of the hospital with responsibility and power devolved. Decentralisation and empowerment therefore were key ingredients in the recipe for success.
- One of the keys to success was the development of a strong sub-unit organisation with service providers given budgetary responsibility. The sub-unit organisation would need management support, including financial management input and regular routine data on activities, budgets and manpower systems.
- A comprehensive information strategy needed to be formulated and adopted prior to taking decisions about data collection and information technology. There was a danger in allowing the development of the process, particularly the information systems, to take place in a fragmented manner.
- It was essential that key groups, nursing, for example, were not marginalised or left to work in isolation.
- The establishment of the ownership of the information used for management was necessary; however, the achievement of this was a slow process.
- It was important not to underestimate development and training needs. A comprehensive training and development

strategy should be part of the fabric of the change process. Well thought out human resource systems were necessary to ensure the success and impact of the project and the involvement of the principal actors.

- Implementing RM required substantial project planning, encompassing information technology implementation, organisational change and training.
- Implementing RM required that, for a period, a parallel management system would be needed. This would involve maintaining the old system until the new systems took over.

CHAPTER 2

The Emergence of Clinical Directorates

Johns Hopkins Hospital

The clinical directorate concept was created in the United States.[15] In 1973, Johns Hopkins Hospital in Baltimore, Maryland introduced a pioneering process of management decentralisation that involved clinicians in the running of the hospital in a structured manner and in the making of corporate decisions. The clinical directorate model was initially conceived as one of a number of cost-cutting measures in response to short-term commercial pressures. It sprang from the realisation that budget management, as in almost all hospitals, was centralised and controlled by executive managers, almost all of whom had no clinical background. But the greater part of the hospital costs resulted from the decisions made by clinicians. There was, therefore, a significant disconnect between financial responsibility and financial decisions.

Johns Hopkins recognised and formalised the financial realities by moving responsibility for operations and finance to the clinical departments and adopting a management structure that gave the clinicians the responsibility for managing costs and controlling resources, thus giving them a major input into both clinical and corporate decision-making. Training was provided to strengthen the management skills of the doctors, and new financial and management information systems were developed to generate the critical data needed to manage the units under the new model.

The Johns Hopkins clinical directorate model was a three-person directorate management team led by a clinician, supported by a director of nursing and a business manager (this is sometimes referred to as the triumvirate model), and was accountable for all service provision and resources.[16] Clinical directorate managers were given considerable autonomy within the parameters of overall hospital policy and strategy. A key factor was achieving the right balance between the different professional disciplines in the clinical directorate. The improved professional and managerial links between budget responsibility and clinical decision-making meant better control of costs and better decisions about allocating resources. No less important, accountability was devolved to where patient care was actually delivered.

A number of factors were critical to the success of the clinical directorates at Johns Hopkins.[17] Executive managers were willing to delegate decision-making and resource control to the clinicians who, in turn, accepted managerial responsibility for the first time. The nursing staff within the hospital supported the new structure and nursing managers were given delegated authority to manage their own resources. New management and financial information systems were developed to support the model.

Within the hospital, a system of effective communication was established between the central unit administration and the unit directorates, and within central and functional areas. The clinical directorate model created at Johns Hopkins was a major innovation in hospital management. It brought about a significant change in culture and forged new and positive relationships between managers and clinicians. The model was quickly adopted by other major US hospitals and attracted considerable international attention as a possible solution for the growing problems of health care costs and the perceived deficiencies of traditional hospital management and the divide between management and clinicians.[18]

Guy's Hospital

In the United Kingdom in the early 1980s, the Johns Hopkins Hospital directorate model was championed by Professor (later Sir) Cyril Chantler of the United Medical and Dental Schools of Guy's and St Thomas' Hospitals.[19] In 1984, spurred by funding restrictions imposed by the resource allocation formula created by the Government's resource allocation working party (RAWP), closure of beds and pay award shortfalls, a group of clinicians and senior managers visited Johns Hopkins to study its decentralised management system. As a result, Guy's was divided into fourteen clinical directorates. Each directorate was headed by a clinical director, usually a doctor, and was supported by a nurse manager and a business manager (the triumvirate model). In some instances, the roles of the business manager and nurse manager were combined, usually into one with a nursing background, but not always (see Figure 1).

Figure 1: Models of Clinical Management

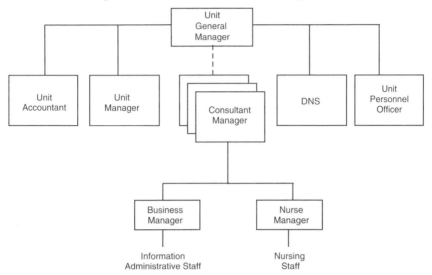

Source: Disken et al. (1990: 22), © Institute of Health Services Management, 1990, reproduced with permission.

The model was taken up by Guy's Hospital and this 'Guy's model' was then seen as the approach to which other flagship NHS trusts should aspire.[20] The 'Guy's model' proposed that clinical services be organised into a series of directorates. Each directorate has a clinical director or lead consultant, usually chosen by the other doctors within the directorate, to act on their behalf. The clinical director is expected to assume responsibility for providing leadership to the directorate and to represent the views of all the clinical specialities. The clinical director is expected to initiate change, agree workloads and resource allocation with the unit general manager, and act as the budget holder for the directorate. The relationship between the clinical director and colleagues is not seen as one of line management. Rather, the clinical director is expected to negotiate with and persuade colleagues. Equally, the relationship between the clinical director and the unit general manager is one of negotiation and persuasion.[21]

In this model, the role of the clinical director is that of part-time manager, continuing to spend most of his or her time on clinical work. Clinical directors are responsible and accountable for planning the service, allocation of resources and operational work.

The nurse manager is managerially accountable to the clinical director and professionally accountable to the director of nursing. Nurses have a key role to play in clinical management. The nurse manager position is usually a senior nurse grade and has the largest day-to-day management role, with responsibility for the operational management of nursing staff, managing the nursing budget, staff development and quality initiatives.

The business manager reports to the clinical director. The business manager is generally responsible for administrative and clerical staff, facilitating the management of directorate affairs and resources, gathering and analysing information, and financial management.

The term 'clinical directorate' is attributed to Professor Chantler, but he subsequently had second thoughts. 'I believe the term "clinical directorate" is unfortunate', he wrote. 'I think I coined the phrase and I wish now that I had not done so. The connotation with authority and command is often unhelpful'.[22] He said that he preferred the usage of the BAMM report,[23] referred to later in this chapter, where 'clinical group' was used to denote the clinical directorate, whilst the 'clinical management team' denoted the team that managed the clinical group. However, in a relatively short period of time, the clinical directorate model (and name) emerged as the accepted model for managing clinical services. Fitzgerald suggested[24] that this popularity was not necessarily related to any hard evidence of the efficacy of the model and that its dissemination might be due to the publicity that the Johns Hopkins Hospital in the US and Guy's Hospital in the UK had received. Whatever the reason, the model was believed to offer the most appropriate way of building on the principles of the Griffiths Inquiry Report in relation to devolution and accountability, and to offer a way of properly engaging medical and other professional staff in the management of NHS trusts.

NHS Reform

The Griffiths Inquiry Report, mentioned in Chapter 1, identified serious weaknesses in NHS management and brought to the fore the concept of general management as a means of improving accountability. The early 1990s saw the pace of NHS reform gather momentum, with a greater emphasis on consumer choice and improvements in quality of service. The *National Health Service Community Care Act, 1990*[25] established a health services internal market by separating the financing and purchasing of care from the provision of care. However, over time the internal market approach slipped out of favour as it became evident it was not contributing to patient choice as had been hoped. The Act also provided for the setting up of self-governing NHS trusts for acute hospitals, mental health services and ambulance services. GPs with large practices were permitted to apply to become fund-holders. Policy emphasis shifted towards the health of the population and giving greater priority to primary care.

In 1998, the consultation document *A First Class Service: Quality in the New NHS*[26] resulted in the introduction of national service frameworks (NSFs), long-term strategies for improving specific areas of care that set measurable goals within set time frames in designated areas such as coronary heart disease, mental health, diabetes, cancer and older people. National clinical directors were given responsibility for the implementation of designated NSFs with the assistance of an external reference group (ERG), which brought together health professionals, service users and carers, health service managers, partner agencies and other advocates. The ERGs are similar to the expert advisory groups (EAGs) set up by the HSE as part of its transformation programme.

The NHS Plan: A Plan for Investment, A Plan for Reform,[27] published in 2000, was accompanied by a significant surge in health service funding. The modernisation agenda that formed the basis of *The NHS Plan* aimed for greater patient and public involvement, opened up the NHS to alternative providers, and established new frameworks for raising performance, standards of care and levels of accountability. Power was shifted closer to the front line. This was supported by training and development for staff as part of a comprehensive new human resource strategy and there was a far greater focus on the use of technology and multidisciplinary working.

The directorate model gradually evolved within the changing NHS as the Government actively sought to involve doctors in a management role and take shared responsibility for resource management issues.[28] The size and format of clinical directorates was left as a matter for local choice and determination. In the early 1990s, some large NHS trusts had elected to have as many as sixteen clinical directorates[29] with the aim of maximising the involvement of senior medical staff in the management of the trust. In these cases, directorates were usually grouped into collectives of directorates sharing a general manager and other administrative functions. The more usual number of directorates, however, was between six and ten, as most organisations felt they could not afford the management costs associated with a greater number of directorates, along with concerns about coordination and control.

Authors writing on clinical directorates[30] have highlighted the following reasons for moving toward a clinical directorate model:

- It provides a structure that gives doctors, nurses and managers responsibility for managing resources
- It facilitates faster decision-making
- It can lead to a reduction of the cost of services
- It can lead to an improvement in the quality of care to patients
- It involves the resource users in solving financial problems associated with resource allocation

Disken et al.[31] highlighted the following reasons for moving into some kind of clinical management:

- Decentralisation and delegation
- To complement rapid developments in information systems
- To pave the way for new information systems
- To break down the barriers between professional hierarchies and groups
- To improve the quality of clinical services to patients
- To reduce the cost of high-cost services
- To bring the consultants 'on board' as a group
- To allow more explicit evaluation of clinical work and outcomes
- To tackle severe financial problems

They went on to say that in most of the hospitals adopting clinical management there was a combination of such reasons, and the rollout programme for resource management had speeded up the process of implementing clinical management structures. Reducing costs alone appeared to have been the primary motivation in very few instances.

The report of Robert J. Maxwell, secretary and chief executive of the King's Fund in the Royal College of Physicians of London, into the role of hospital consultants in clinical directorates[32] suggested the following guidelines for a successful directorate:

- The number of directorates needed to be sufficient to reflect the real variety of clinical activity
- There must be commitment from both the medical and nursing professions and general management
- Clinical directors must have authority to deal with problems within their directorate
- Clinical directorates must meet their targets
- Information on performance and expenditure must be accurate and timely but not over-elaborate
- Clinical directors were there to lead, not to manage. Their role and the role of the other leaders – the nurse manager and business manager – must be clear

Caroline Rea stated[33] that the clinical directorate model offers the advantage of:

- A structure where doctors, nurses and managers manage a clinical service
- Decision-making that is closer to the patient and therefore more responsive
- Breaking down of professional barriers
- More relevant and accurate information
- More effective budgetary control

In discussing the long-term future of clinical directorates and addressing the question will they work in the future?, Caroline Rea,[34] writing in 1995, noted that there was a danger that clinical directorates could become the new power bases, strong and self-interested, and not take account of wider hospital issues. With the clinical directorate model, it is difficult to hold the institution together as a unit with shared identity and vision. Coordination and integration across directorates can be difficult. There is also the possibility of increased inefficiencies associated with the provision of services to and the support for several small management teams, for example, in finance and personnel services. However, despite these problems, the model has continued to attract considerable support from organisations and individuals. It appears to have an internal logic based on the need to involve users in decision-making and in the wider trend towards quality and efficiency being generated by the people who do things knowing what needs to be done and working out how to do it rather than just being told.

Disken et al.[35] looked at the different working relationships within the clinical directorate model:

- In the clinical director–consultant relationship, the concern of consultants is clinical freedom. No other person can instruct a consultant how to clinically treat patients once patients are treated in accordance with standards, ethics, resources, etc. The clinical director must have the support and confidence of his or her colleagues.
- Clinical directors are described as managers of the core staff, including nursing and business. In practice, nurse managers and business managers do not see clinical directors as their 'full' managers and retain professional accountability links outside the directorate. The clinical director is seen as lead coordinator of the team.
- Most models suggest that the clinical director is accountable to the chief executive officer (CEO). In practice, their relationship is one of colleagues working together. It is a negotiated and mutually agreed relationship.
- In most instances, nurses retain their relationship (dotted line on the organisation chart) with the director of nursing services (DNS), whose role is one of professional responsibility for nursing. It is important that these relationships are clearly defined, as split loyalties and confusion can result.

In 1993, the British Association of Medical Managers (BAMM), the British Medical Association (BMA), the Institute of Health Services Management (IHSM) and the Royal College of Nursing (RCN) produced *Managing Clinical Services: A Consensus Statement of Principles for Effective Clinical Management*, referred to as the BAMM report,[36] which was based on a survey that tapped into the experiences of practitioners and sought to find out what worked and what did not. In relation to the question of roles, clinical management team (CMT) members were asked how they perceived their own influence on a set of common tasks. Clinical directors, with the support of business managers, had a strong influence over strategic planning within the clinical group. Clinical directors and nurse managers had a lead influence over setting standards, with the nurse manager having a lead influence over monitoring them. Clinical directors and nurse managers had little or no influence over the size of the clinical group budget, while business managers had major or moderate influence. No CMT member had more than 20 per cent major influence over information systems. No clear patterns of influence for individual roles emerged, with no one member of the CMT having a dominant role.

The survey said that CMT members had training and development needs in areas such as financial management, marketing, information management and change management. But there was a low level of investment in meeting these needs. Heads of clinical services prioritised the same areas, with the addition of managing upward. The results showed that almost everyone in the CMTs felt unprepared to do the job. The survey said that chief executives needed to make a real commitment of resources to the development of staff, to enhance their knowledge and skills to enable them to fulfil their role.

Edmondstone and Chisnell[37] also referred to the need for training and development programmes for members of the CMTs in areas such as:

- Financial management
- Information management
- Leading and working in teams
- Change management
- Persuading, influencing and negotiating skills

Training and development took on greater importance in the light of the fact that early experiences of appointing CMTs indicated that the complexity of roles had not been not fully understood, often resulting in junior managers being appointed. This had now changed, with more experienced nurse and business managers being appointed. It was only in this way, said the report, that effective clinical management within the directorate could be achieved.

The BAMM report also helped define the characteristics of effective clinical management:

- Progressively improving and explicitly developing approaches to quality in health care, efficiency and effectiveness of patient care
- Creating an environment in which all staff in a clinical group can innovate, take risks and feel empowered to act to improve patient care

- Making decisions on the use of resources explicit and consistent with defined goals
- Contributing to the development, understanding and implementation of shared corporate goals, both within the individual clinical group and the hospital as a whole
- Fully exploiting the skills and experience of the clinical management team members
- Promoting the culture of investment in the education, training and development of the members of the clinical group and of the clinical management team
- Ensuring the availability of accurate, timely, patient-based information to support the process and create a culture of decision-making based on this information

The most important factor in making clinical management effective is teamwork. The work of the CMT is multidisciplinary in nature. The triumvirate model requires the three people to work closely together and have confidence in each other's ability. It also means that interdependence is necessary for the effectiveness of the team. Team building requires openness and respect. This places considerable stress and importance on the development of relationships and communications. It also requires people of some experience and maturity.

Disken et al. highlighted[38] concern over the rapid turnover of nurse managers and business managers, with consequent loss of continuity. The development of career paths needed to be reviewed in the light of greater seniority and rewards within their clinical management roles. For the nurse manager, one option is director of nursing. An alternative option is general management. For the business manager, one option is from a smaller directorate to larger, more complex ones and then further into general management. The transition of staff into the role of nurse manager and business manager suggests the need for locally based guidance, training and support to ensure effective management of the clinical directorate.

The role of the director of nursing in a clinical directorate setting has undergone considerable change. Traditionally, nurse managers answered to the director of nursing in their functional capacity. In a clinical directorate model, that is no longer true. The director of nursing now has a new role,[39] accountable to the CEO for the strategic planning of nursing and midwifery services, standard setting, monitoring and evaluating nursing services and providing leadership and professional development expertise to nursing staff. The role is more one of managing nursing rather than nurses.

The BAMM report showed that the director of nursing commonly has lead responsibility within a hospital for quality management, which involves innovation and coordination of activities within and between clinical groups. The director of nursing role in clinical management organisations provides an opportunity to develop a new way of working. The management style shifts from direction to facilitation. The role is one of development, working alongside nurse managers to empower them, and, through them, empowering the patient. This change, allied with a commitment to multidisciplinary work and an explicit quality brief, combines to form a powerful tool for increasing responsiveness to patients' needs.

The relationship between the senior nurse within a directorate and the director of nursing at board level was explicitly stated by the Royal College of Nursing[40] to mean accountability for particular things, exercised in particular ways. According to the RCN, the senior nurse is accountable to the director of nursing for:

- Ensuring that standards of nursing within the directorate conform with good practice defined by the profession as a whole and with the standards set by the profession within the organisation and agreed at board level
- Ensuring compliance with statutory nursing obligations within the directorate
- Facilitating the development of nursing practice within the directorate in line with nationally and locally agreed policies and strategies for nursing
- Ensuring the development and continuing education of all nurses working within the directorate

The BAMM report also highlighted that, within the directorate management structure, there is the question of the service of professionals allied to medicine (PAMs), who include dieticians, physiotherapists, occupational therapists, radiographers, pharmacists and others. It is important to understand how they are affected by the clinical directorate structure in order to ensure that they have a voice in corporate decision-making. In some instances, they form their own clinical group, with one of the professional heads becoming clinical director. This model has the advantage of professional heads being responsible for the line management of their staff. Alternatively, the PAMs services are managed within a directorate, under the line management of one of the clinical management team. While this model encourages multidisciplinary work and gives the directorate control over resources, it isolates the practitioners from their peer group and the question of monitoring of professional standards needs to be addressed.

In a keynote address to the Institute of Health Services Management Conference,[41] Robert J. Maxwell described the clinical directorate structure as the bridge or hinge between management of clinical activity in health services and management of the institution. Management is not an exact science. There is a degree of fuzziness about it. It is more experience-based and more an art form. A manager's performance might be assessed by the effect he or she is having on others and on the organisation. A manager might, for example, be able to develop a good team, resolve crises, avoid crises and deal with risk management. Management of clinical services is not just about maintaining a budget.

Romesh Gupta and colleagues[42] conducted a survey of consultants in the UK in 2006 to examine their views on, and evaluate the effectiveness of, the clinical directorate system. Approximately one-third of respondents had current or past clinical directorate experience and the other two-thirds had none. The survey showed that most consultants wished to see the clinical directorate system continue, but in a modified form. Asked for their views on the future of the clinical directorate system, there was a wide difference between consultants with and without experience. Most consultants with experience wished to see the current system retained (34 per cent) or modified (28 per cent), as against those who preferred to see the system replaced (9 percent) or scrapped (25 per cent). The rest did not respond to the question. Among consultants without experience, 15 per cent wished it to be retained, 55 per cent said it should be modified and 24 per cent believed it should be replaced or scrapped. Six per cent did not respond to the question.

Respondents were asked if they considered that they were actively involved in decision-making as well as being fully participating stakeholders in the delivery of the service. Only one-third (mostly those with experience) gave a positive response, with just under one-half stating that they did not believe that they played any important role in the decision-making or the shaping of services and that their views were not considered. Most clinical directors were positive about their role in communicating with their colleagues. Non-clinical director respondents were less in agreement. In fact, half of all respondents felt that clinical directors only communicated management decisions to their colleagues; just about one-third saw the clinical director as a link between management and their fellow consultants.

These views seem to reflect a frustration and lack of confidence in the system by some consultants, who were of the view that most decisions were target-focused and politically driven. They believed that most current clinical directors had neither the authority nor the experience to resist management pressure to prioritise these agendas. This confirmed a view expressed earlier by Romesh Gupta[43] that there was a perception that clinical directors had been used only for downward communication from management and had not developed the partnership between management and clinicians that was the basis of the clinical directorate concept. This is not always an easy task. Clinical directors tend to find the role of mediator between management and clinical colleagues both demanding and stressful.[44] M.L. Thorne provocatively asked, 'is the clinical director first among equals or just a go between?'[45]

Gupta et al.[46] concluded from their survey that experienced consultants should be preferred over younger colleagues for the position of clinical director, who should preferably be the choice of consultants rather than management. The clinical director needed to be 'a true bridge' between consultants and management and represent the views of both. The authors were of the opinion that, with an enhanced engagement of consultants, morale would improve and positively influence patient care through a stronger partnership with management.

Learning from the NHS

The establishment of the NHS and the creation of the welfare state in Britain provided a stimulus for the Irish Government to examine the possibility of introducing similar arrangements in Ireland.[47] In 1947, a white paper, *Outline of Proposals for the Improvement of the Health Services,*[48] proposed an Irish version of the NHS and a further white paper, *Social Security,*[49] published in 1949, put forward a system of national social insurance for all. The health proposal collapsed in controversy as a result of sustained opposition from, among others, the Church and the medical profession. The social insurance proposal was dropped on the basis that Ireland could not afford it. Thereafter, until the 1990s, improvements in both health and social welfare were incremental and tended to be ad hoc rather than strategic. While recognising that the UK health services model could not be adopted in Ireland, the Irish Government continued to closely observe what was happening in UK health policy and the development of the NHS to see what reference they might have to the Irish health services. This acquired added impetus with the launch of the health service reform programme (HSRP)[50] in Ireland.

In Ireland, the Office for Health Management (OHM) commissioned the Office for Public Management (OPM) to review how the UK experience of health reform could assist strategic planning and organisational development in the Irish health services. The results of this study were published in 2003 in a report, *Learning from the NHS in Change*,[51] which highlighted five key lessons in relation to the involvement of clinicians in management.

First, it was important to consider how the complex dynamics of change were handled, and how the human consequences of these actions were managed. The importance of engaging people could not be overestimated and this was especially clear in relation to the involvement of clinicians and others on the front line: their active engagement in the process of reform had been a vital element in transforming NHS services.

Second, effective change management required clearly articulated values and a shared purpose. Realistic time frames, with identifiable milestones along the way, were also required so that people could see the evidence of emerging benefits and feel confident about the direction in which they were going.

Third, a clear human resources (HR) strategy, with a realistic investment in leadership and management development, was essential in delivering major organisational change in health services.

Fourth, it was important to get the infrastructure right; this included building the workforce capacity, encouraging organisational agility and flexibility, and developing the technology and information systems required to support service improvement.

Fifth, people recognised the value of having an agency dedicated to promoting reform and modernisation through leadership and service improvement programmes, firmly linked to change objectives. However, central leadership and direction must be balanced with the need to encourage local ownership and innovation. Service improvement and performance management outcomes should have meaning both across the system and within local health economies.

The report identified a number of implications for involving clinicians in a management role in Ireland's health services:

- Reconfiguration needed to start with the strategic vision for change and modelling the infrastructure requirements as soon as possible. This required new methodologies, particularly for workforce modelling, away from the 'silo' professional culture, and into mapping networks of care – with tasks rather than particular professions. This, however, required early buy-in from the professional associations or colleges and training establishments.
- A drive to engage the clinician around professional – and therefore accountable – practice was needed to inform and integrate change.
- The potential of teamworking to capture and share learning and drive local change needed to be exploited.
- It was necessary to work with whole systems approaches, such as the care pathways, which involve multi-professional teams and cross-organisational working.
- Should the Irish system remain a mixed economy of providers, it was vital to get right the issue of health care governance (clinical and corporate) across one system; the risk of small and unrelated scrutiny and governance units should be minimised.

The report quoted from a 2001 review commissioned by the NHS service delivery and organisation (SDO) national research and development (R&D) programme, *Managing Change in the NHS*,[52] which argued that the purely top-down, imposed approach of re-engineering had not proved successful in the NHS. Both bottom-up commitment, including the initiative of clinicians, and senior leadership were key to ensuring that smaller improvements were consistent with overall direction. It was also vital for ensuring that redesign initiatives were integrated with mainstream organisational processes and objectives. While it was extremely helpful to have a dedicated change team that could maintain momentum and provide a pool of expertise, it was important that the team was not dismissed as a 'special project'. The review said that that redesign takes time, and that hopes of 'overnight' transformation were misplaced, although identifying some early successes helped gain interest and acceptance. Individuals and organisations needed time to learn new ways of thinking, to reflect and to implement, and both clinical and managerial staff needed to dedicate and set aside time to do this.

CHAPTER 3

Early Examples of the Implementation of Clinical Directorates

Introduction

The first examples of clinical directorates in Ireland emerged in the early part of the 1990s. At the forefront of developments were hospitals such as St James's Hospital in Dublin, Cork University Hospital, Galway University Hospital and Waterford Regional Hospital. In March 1992, St James's Hospital, Dublin asked the then Department of Health to approve a proposal for the institution of a major organisational and management structural change project at the hospital. The broad thrust of the project was to change the structure of the hospital from a predominantly centralised, hierarchical and functional structure to a decentralised, flat and product-/service-focused structure with a market orientation. One of the central structural platforms on which this change programme was based was the clinical directorate model. In approving the proposal, the Department stated that, in addition to addressing the strategic and organisational needs of St James's, the proposed initiative would have significance in the much wider context of Irish hospital and health services management in general.

At that time, the author was employed as nurse manager in the CResT Clinical Directorate (cardiology, respiratory medicine, cardiothoracic surgery, palliative care, pharmacology, and therapeutics and vascular surgery) in St James's Hospital, and, in 1995, carried out a research study of five hospital sites that were also in the early stages of developing clinical directorates.[53] Three of these hospitals were in England (Milton Keynes, Birmingham Heartlands, and Guy's and St Thomas') one in Northern Ireland (the Royal Victoria Hospital, Belfast) and one in the Republic of Ireland (Cork University Hospital). The study included visits to the five sites and interviews with thirty-four chief executives, directors of nursing, clinical directors, nurse managers, business managers, ward sisters and personnel managers and others. The early experience of clinical directorates in St James's, together with the results of the survey, provide a useful comparative insight into the operational details involved in the way in which clinical directorates were developing in Ireland and the UK at the time. Many of the operational issues raised are relevant today.

Hospitals Surveyed

The choice of hospitals for interview was based on a desire to examine a range of different approaches to the introduction of clinical management structures. Three of the five started with the triumvirate model of clinical director, nurse manager and business manager, while another had a clinical director, business manager and ward sister model. The fifth site commenced with service managers only, as the medical consultants had not as yet decided to participate. Three principal reasons were given for the delay in participation in the directorate system by consultants: 1) the perception that a project manager responsible for implementing the system had been imposed from outside the region without consultation, 2) the lack of consultation in general with consultants about the most appropriate system and structure, and 3) the apparent inability of the project manager to adapt the general model of a clinical directorate to the cultural and structural idiosyncrasies of the region.

In a number of the sites, some structural changes involved combining the two roles of nurse manager and business manager (renamed directorate manager), and a person from a nursing background did not necessarily always fill this new post. A senior nurse was always appointed to assist the directorate manager. This change of structure tended to happen when clinical directorates were getting stronger and more self-assured, and was imposed centrally, often against the wishes of team members, ostensibly to achieve a clearer definition of roles within the directorate and trim down the structure. This created tension within the team. In some instances the reporting relationship changed, with the nurse manager reporting to the directorate manager. In one site, the nurse managers refused to cooperate and clinical directors insisted on maintaining a direct reporting relationship. The difficulties experienced are encapsulated in a comment from one of the interviews: 'Nurses are marginalised within the clinical directorate system.'

Two sites introduced a senior manager across a number of directorates to support the group/clinical director. This was seen as an important communications link between the executive and the directorate staff. However, the introduction of additional layers of management seem to contradict the original concept of the clinical directorate as a flatter, de-layered management structure, as was highlighted by one of the interviewees:

> It creates too many managers. With directorate managers and clinical operational managers the power of the clinical director is cut, yet he still has the same responsibility. There is also a danger of de-professionalising health care workers.

The restructuring of clinical directorates took place with the development of a group structure on two sites to achieve better clinical cohesiveness, coordination and decision-making at executive level. Resistance by clinical directors in one site prevented this from happening. On two sites, senior nurses were not appointed for some time. This resulted in the quality and standards of patient care suffering and low morale at clinical (nursing) level. The intention had been to achieve a substantial devolvement of authority and power at sister level. However, there was no support provided to the sisters, who felt that they lacked leadership in areas such as quality and development. These sites were proceeding with the appointment of senior nurses.

St James's Hospital

St James's Hospital, which dates back to 1702, was originally a foundling hospital and, over the years, underwent a number of changes and transformations. By the 1950s it had become very much a hospital for Dublin's working-class people. St James's Hospital Board was established under the *Health (Corporate Bodies) Act 1961*[54] and the *St James's Hospital Board (Establishment Orders) 1971* and *1984.*[55] The ethos and thinking behind the Act came from the *Fitzgerald Report,*[56] which recommended the creation of a network of general hospitals to underpin the provision of health services. St James's was one of the recommended sites. As part of a policy of hospital rationalisation, four Dublin hospitals – Mercer's, Sir Patrick Dun's, Baggot St and Dr Steevens' – closed for acute services in 1986/1987 and the bulk of their services were transferred to St James's. This fact is important in understanding many of the issues that faced the hospital as it embarked on a programme of renewal and change.

In late 1993, two pilot clinical directorates were established in St James's Hospital. One was in cardiology, respiratory medicine and thoracic surgery and became known as the CReST directorate. The second was in medicine for the elderly and became known as the MedEL directorate. A third directorate, the ORIAN directorate, was established in 1995, and was comprised of operating rooms, a general intensive care unit, a high dependency unit, a day surgical unit, a laser unit, an endovascular unit, a sterile supplies unit and anaesthetics. A directorate management team was appointed for each, consisting of a clinical director, a nurse manager and a business manager. The three clinical directors became members of the executive management group (EMG) of the hospital. The longer-term intention (which was achieved) was to establish nine clinical directorates within the hospital and four support directorates. These directorates would function within a structure that was decentralised and divided into a corporate and a services division.

At senior management level within the hospital, the deputy chief executive was responsible for the implementation of the project for establishing clinical directorates throughout the hospital. A project manager was responsible for the planning and implementation, with a project assistant providing support to the clinical directorates.

Planning for the new structure in St James's was contained in a series of documents that defined an organisation that would be decentralised, flat-structured and product-focused, with a market bias. The documents were:

- *Proposal to Pilot an Organisation and Management Structure Change Project:*[57] this was the original document that was submitted to the Department of Health requesting financial assistance to embark on the change programme.
- *Sample Clinical Directorate Configurations:*[58] this set out some alternative configurations for clinical directorates and support directorates.
- *Clinical Directorate Project Implementation Plan: Key Tasks:*[59] this was a comprehensive road map for charting progress through the change project.
- *Project Implementation Plan:*[60] this specified the need for individual project implementation plans from each of the emerging clinical directorates.
- *Accounting and Information Support for Clinical Directorates: Framework for Development:*[61] considerable attention was given to

information systems in resource management within St James's and this document provided a framework for developing information systems.

- A *Project Evaluation Framework*[62] was prepared in 1995 to provide a basis for measurement of progress, success and failure for the change management project.
- *Terms of Reference*[63] were drawn up for application user groups, which were formed to ensure involvement of key personnel.

At that time, the board of St James's Hospital made and directed policy with regard to the wishes expressed by the Minister and delegated the management function to the CEO. The board was also linked in an informal policymaking way to an executive management group (EMG) and a clinical management group (CMG). The EMG comprised the CEO, operations manager/deputy CEO, director of nursing, financial manager, personnel manager, information and management services manager, general support services manager and the clinical directors. The EMG met fortnightly and made corporate executive decisions. The hospital was divided functionally into two major divisions: corporate and services. The corporate division encompassed functions that were horizontal across the hospital and was managed by the financial manager, personnel manager, information and management services manager and technical services estate manager. Each reported directly to the CEO.

In the new structure introduced in 1993, the director of nursing, reporting directly to the CEO, had overall corporate responsibility for quality throughout the hospital. This included case-mix, risk management, standards and utilisation review. The director of nursing continued to have line management responsibility for the school of nursing. Line management responsibility for nursing staff under the new structure was transferred to the nurse manager within the directorates. During the period of transition, the director of nursing, through the assistant directors of nursing, continued to have line management responsibility for non-directorate nursing staff and also had a professional link to the nurse managers within the directorates.

Within this new structure, the services division comprised the nine clinical directorates and four clinical support directorates. The functional areas of medical administration (secretariat, medical records, consultant establishment setting, non-consultant hospital doctors, patient property) and scientific (physics, bio-engineering, pharmacy) were managed by the deputy CEO/operations manager, with departmental heads reporting directly to him. The general support services manager had responsibility for general support service areas, with departmental heads reporting directly to him. The clinical directors, deputy CEO/operations manager, director of nursing and general support services manager all reported directly to the CEO.

In general, clinical directorates management was involved in the selection of directorate staff, with recruitment of lower grades of staff being carried out centrally. The director of nursing was involved in the selection of senior nursing personnel, with the personnel department carrying out the administrative role. The directorates had a specified person in the personnel department with whom to liaise.

While the roles of the clinical director, nurse manager and business manager were critical to the success of the directorate model at St James's, it is important also to take into account other roles within the hospital. PAMs, such as paramedical staff, also had a voice in corporate decision-making. This had the advantage of professional heads being responsible for line management of their staff and ensuring monitoring of professional standards.

The Clinical Management Team

Clinical Director
In the new structure in St James's, the clinical director was accountable to the CEO and, as in other hospitals in the UK, had a three-year contract of appointment. The CEO was involved in the selection of clinical directors, with agreement from consultant staff in the group. The clinical director represented the clinical management team at EMG meetings and had overall responsibility for the management of all staff in the directorate. In practice, the management of nursing staff was delegated to the nurse manager and non-medical staff to the business manager. The clinical director was also responsible for the development and execution of business plans and would assist in the design of accounting and information structures and the development of clinical protocols and in developing and implementing effective mechanisms for medical audits.

Succession planning is a significant problem at clinical director level. A number of the hospital sites visited showed a lack of consultants willing to take on the clinical director's role, with, in one case, consultants refusing to cooperate and, in another, the position of clinical director rotating every three months because people were not willing to take it on full-time. In the St James's interviews, some of the reasons mentioned for this reluctance by consultants to become a clinical director included a perception by consultants that they would be at a financial loss, their teaching and research would suffer and there was no exit mechanism for clinical directors. It should not be assumed that, because consultants were good doctors, they would make good managers. The consultant needed to learn about the clinical directorate system. One interviewee pointed out that consultants spend a long time training to be a specialist and were then being asked to take on a different role with no training. Were they, he asked, interested in being 'amateur managers' for the rest of their career?

The survey of the five hospitals showed general agreement in all of the sites about the role of the clinical director, who was accountable to the chief executive or group director as appropriate. He or she represented the clinical management team at executive and board levels and had overall responsibility for managing all staff in the directorate. In practice, the management of non-medical staff was delegated to the nurse manager, business manager or directorate manager. The clinical director was also responsible for coordinating business plans and service developments and had overall responsibility for business plans and budgets, with appropriate devolvement and delegation. He or she was also usually responsible for developing effective mechanisms for medical and clinical auditing and was also responsible for staff training and development, and appraisal and monitoring of work.

It was not always the case that a good consultant would make a good clinical director. Some interviewees expressed concern about the difficulty of ensuring that clinical directors had the requisite skills to be good managers:

> Consultants are mainly interested in clinical work. Very few doctors are good managers.

> Clinical directors are part-time managers who are doctors and not trained in management.

Nurse Manager
The nurse manager in St James's was managerially accountable to the clinical director and professionally accountable to the director of

nursing and was responsible for the operational management of nursing and allied staff and, therefore, had executive responsibility for managing the nursing resources. The nurse manager participated in the development and implementation of the directorate business plan and was involved in budgetary preparation from the perspective of nursing resource requirements. The nurse manager was also expected to participate in the design of accounting and information systems necessary for the directorate and was responsible for the performance appraisal of nursing staff and for the ongoing education of nursing and allied staff. With two of the three business managers in the St James's directorates having a nursing background, this represented a significant enhancement of career opportunities for nurses.

Detached from the traditional support mechanisms, some nurse managers seemed to have had difficulty in adjusting to their new role. Some of the hospitals visited had rapid turnover and experienced other difficulties with this post (as well as that of the business manager). Within the St James's directorates, two nurse managers had departed at an early stage. One problem seemed to be marginalisation of nurse managers within the system. Information technology and finance had a higher level of priority and enjoyed a higher corporate profile, despite the fact that clinical directorates were meant to be about better patient care and this care was coordinated and delivered on a twenty-four-hour basis by the nurses. Within the directorates, the nurse manager had the bigger personnel management responsibility to carry and, consequently, also was accountable for a high pay budget. He or she was also responsible for standards of care and nursing development and for the development of the nursing staff. These roles required the development of new skills and a high degree of assertiveness within the clinical management team of the directorate. The calibre of the nurse manager, therefore, was crucial in making the directorate system work.

In the survey of the five hospital sites, there also appeared to be general agreement about the role of the nurse manager in all sites. The nurse manager was managerially accountable to the clinical director or directorate manager, depending on the structure of the clinical management team, and was professionally accountable to the director of nursing and quality. In the UK, the role of the director of nursing was changing and was increasingly becoming one that encompassed the dual function of professional responsibility for nursing and overall responsibility for quality initiatives within the hospital. The role of the nurse manager within the directorates usually involved leading nursing practice developments and quality initiatives, managing the nursing budget, day-to-day management of the operational aspects of nursing and performance appraisal and training and development of nursing staff.

The introduction of the directorate structure had significant implications for the role of the director of nursing and the role had undergone major change in all of the sites visited. He or she was now accountable to the CEO, was seen as the professional head of nursing and was also emerging as the principal officer within the hospital for all quality assurance initiatives.

Business Manager

In St James's, the business manager was accountable to the clinical director. His or her responsibilities usually included managing clerical staff, management of the directorate office, business planning support, finance, identifying information needs and analysing information. The business manager was managerially accountable to the clinical director and professionally accountable to the deputy CEO/operations manager. He or she had operational management responsibility for clerical staff and had budget control of delegated areas. The business manager participated in directorate business plan and budgetary bid preparation, in the design of accounting and information systems and in the collection, collation and analysis of information. The business manager was responsible for training and development of clerical/administrative and non-medical/non-nursing staff.

Business managers, like nurse managers, experienced a sense of isolation in their new roles. In other sites, the trend had been for business managers to cover more than one directorate. It was apparent that, while there was a lot of work to be done at the early stages of implementing the directorates, the role of the business manager became largely advisory and one of monitoring once the systems had been designed and implemented, especially with IT and finance. For the business manager and the nurse manager, therefore, there were significant skill development issues and a significant requirement for ongoing training and development. This issue was particularly highlighted by the BAMM report,[64] which indicated that most members of the clinical management teams felt unprepared for their new roles. The BAMM report also highlighted that the complexity of these roles was usually not well understood within hospitals at the beginning of the RM process. Often junior managers were appointed to the posts with negative results and this subsequently had to be changed, with the appointment of more experienced and better-qualified individuals.

The survey of hospital sites identified four other roles:

Directorate Manager

Accountable to the clinical director, the role of the directorate mana-ger combined the responsibilities of the business manager and the nurse manager, although he or she was usually supported by a senior nurse who took responsibility for the day-to-day management of the nursing operations. Duties usually included providing leadership to directorate staff, formulating and implementing business plans, developing and implementing information systems, budget management, service development and overall responsi-bility for training and development within the directorate.

Service Manager

The role of the service manager was very similar to that of the directorate manager. It was a combined function, encompassing the roles of the business manager and nurse manager. The difference however was that, in bed-holding areas, the role was usually filled by a senior nurse and there was no additional senior nurse manager. He or she was also accountable to the clinical director and the CEO and, in this, the role also differed from that of the directorate manager, who was solely answerable to the clinical director. This system was particular to one hospital that had only begun the process of implementing the clinical directorate system. The directorate manager's role emerged in the UK in apparent response to the changing demands of the contracting system and the increased level of commercial responsibility being placed on the shoulders of the holder of this post by the demands of this system. The services manager role was firmly located within the structure of the Irish health care system and, more particularly, within the structure of the then health boards, and, subsequently, the HSE.

Director of Nursing/Quality

The introduction of the directorate structure had significant implications for the role of the director of nursing and the role had undergone major change in all of the sites visited. He or she was now accountable to the CEO, was seen as the professional head of nursing and was also emerging as the principal officer within the hospital for all quality assurance initiatives.

Group Director

A number of the sites visited had begun to create group directorates – a number of clinical directorates grouped together with a view to introducing some element of rationalisation and cohesion into the structure. For example, instead of having up to twenty-seven clinical directors at an executive management meeting, only six group directors were necessary. The group director was usually a consultant, was accountable to the CEO, and coordinated the management of the clinical directorates while respecting the independence and clinical autonomy of the individual clinical directors. The principal duty was to represent the directorates at executive management level. He or she was usually offered a three-year appointment.

Main Features of Clinical Directorates

Information Systems

Information management was at the heart of the change process within St James's Hospital. An extensive study of information requirements within the hospital, both present and future, was completed in 1992 and culminated in the launch of a new hospital information system programme, the *St James's Hospital Total Hospital Information Systems Strategic Plan*.[65] It was a major landmark for modern change at St James's Hospital, marking as it did the culmination of three years of extensive planning and evaluation, in which all levels of staff had participated. It also marked the beginning of a three-year implementation plan to deliver a comprehensive modern information system to the hospital. The task of achieving this was the responsibility of the information and management services department (IMS).

Within the strategic plan, IMS stated that its mission was to provide an effective information systems framework capable of supporting the information and management services needs of St James's Hospital, necessary to fulfil its mission.[66] The mission of the hospital, which was contained in the plan, was to provide high quality, cost-effective facilities in the following areas: patient care delivery (local, regional, national); education (medical, dental, nursing and paramedical); and research and development (clinical and basic scientific).[67]

In order to achieve its mission, IMS developed the following set of goals and objectives:[68]

- Establish and maintain a common hospital information database, incorporating basic task support and decision support systems, to enable all clinical service units to function in an integrated and efficient manner
- Develop IT facilities to support the hospital's education and training functions
- Develop methods, tools and IT facilities to support the R&D programme, and to contribute to the development of hospital-wide medical informatics
- Establish and develop an integrated patient information system to record a patient care profile, sufficient to enable each stage of patient care to proceed without delay. Areas of specific impact to patient flow are admission and registration, investigation and diagnosis, and therapy and treatment
- Establish and develop a comprehensive resource utilisation and planning information system to facilitate the calculation of service unit costs and the forecasting of service demands
- Establish and develop budgetary control, financial and manpower management systems (a) to enable budget holders to monitor and control day-to-day finances and staffing, and (b) to generate a management information database to facilitate the effective planning, management and control of resources
- Establish and develop management sciences information systems and facilities to support the planning and decision-making processes and to provide performance feedback on key aspects of service activity

In the survey of the five hospital sites, adequacy of information systems varied considerably. All had a combination of manual and computerised systems at different stages of development. Two sites had a case-mix database with a patient administrative system (PAS), pathology, radiology, theatres and pharmacy (partially used only for expensive drugs and certain areas) feeding data to the database. In all sites, this case-mix system held activity data only.

Another site installed a clinical information system (CIS) in 1990, with the principal objective of giving clinicians access to a comprehensive range of information expressed in clinical and financial terms. The computerisation of this did not go smoothly. The basic hospital system, which was to act as host to the CIS, was not good enough to take information from the CIS. Large parts of the hospital were unable to key in data upon which reports could be generated. In areas where terminals were installed, the data produced from the CIS was questionable. Many of the feeder systems such as pharmacy and theatre were still being entered manually.

The information deficiencies became clear with the introduction of contracts and GP fund holding in the UK in 1993. Some of the reasons for the problems were that not all medical staff were made aware of the importance of coding, there was a devolution of the medical records function, with no additional staff being employed as coding clerks, the capacity of the central processing unit was too small and, finally, IT was frequently seen as *the* solution, without sufficient emphasis on the need for good report generation. One chief executive said that the exercise had cost too much and he would not do it again. In order to tackle some of the problems, a director of corporate information was appointed to ensure that all patient-related information was captured and properly coded. Another site was piloting a case-mix system with information from the PAS feeding into the system. A multi-area site had a PAS in place in one of the hospital areas for a number of years, with an IMS manager developing the system.

Most sites collected core data from feeders, mainly PAS, with other feeder systems at different stages of development. Across the sites, there was an emphasis on activity data and ensuring that the data was accurate. Recording of procedures and diagnoses was carried out by medical secretaries or by clinical coding staff. Three of the sites had invested in nursing systems. Off-the-shelf packages were used and modified. Despite much effort and time, results were reportedly disappointing. One site that had the system switched it off because of technical and user problems and because the staff said that the system lacked relevance to their work. Care planning took more time than their former manual system. During busy periods, recording of activity was not completed and, therefore, the hospital did not have an accurate recording system. Staff had to start from scratch and revert to the hand-written care-planning system that had been abandoned. Another site switched off the dependency part of the nursing system because the staff requirements (planned versus actual) were so high. A third site was piloting a system but was having similar problems. A fourth site did some preparatory work on care plans for computerisation but decided not to invest further.

Each site had an IT payroll system. None had an IT personnel system. Line managers were recording absenteeism manually. There was a variety of manual and computerised systems in place to assist in managing resources on a day-to-day basis. With one exception, ordering of supplies was done manually, with individual cost centres and codes for users. Pharmacy systems were mainly used for stock control and general ward costings. On one site, expensive drugs were costed to individual patients, and the system was used to keep patient medication records in the oncology and drug dependency unit. Computerised prescribing was not then available.

The information systems being developed on the sites at the time were designed to support the work of the clinical directorates. All had a central IT team to manage the size and functions of the systems and they played a crucial role in developing the systems and in training and supporting staff in the clinical directorates. Reports generated on a routine basis consisted mainly of summary activity data and this information was used for capital planning, occupancy levels, trends planning and, in the UK, for the management of contracts.

Finance

There was an increasing emphasis on linking costs to activity. The NHS reforms of 1990[69] represented a major change in organising and financing the service. The separation of the purchaser/provider role formed the basis of the then contracting process, in which district health authorities purchased services to meet the health needs of their population.[70] Regional health authorities and GP fund holders also purchased services.

Two of the sites interviewed had centralised business units (separate from the clinical directorates) that dealt with the bulk of the contracts. At other sites, the clinical directorates received assistance from hospital accountants. Business planning guidelines were issued to the directorates from the business unit, chief executive or chief financial officer. A draft business plan with prices of procedures, which included labour, consumables and length of stay, was discussed with the director of finance and the CEO within the hospital; responsibility for volume, activity, quality and cost lay within the clinical directorates. Across the UK sites, activities and costs were agreed between purchasers and providers. Business planning took place at both directorate level and corporate level. Clinical directorates usually received a rollover budget to pay for items such as pay, consumables and other items. The capital budget was held centrally. Budget accountability in all sites rested with the clinical director, who delegated this to the business and nurse managers. On two sites, budgets had been devolved to some ward sisters, who received budgetary information, were involved in setting the budget and made decisions regarding their own skill mix, while the senior nurse/nurse manager had overall budgetary accountability. If bigger budgets were required, these were negotiated between the ward sister, the nurse manager, the business manager and the accountant. On one site, budgets had been devolved to all ward sisters, who had overall budgetary accountability.

Initially, directorates that over-spent were bailed out, but this changed, with over-spenders required to carry the over-spend into the following years' budgets. In some instances, over-spends were outside the control of the directorate and a case had to be made to the chief executive. Additional pressure on clinical directorates that over-spent came from other clinical directorates that were keeping within budget. Future bailing-out of the over-spenders meant a diminution in their share of the cake. Clinical directorates that under-spent had to give the surplus to a central fund that was used to finance deficits. When the Government demanded savings from an organisation, general management usually negotiated individually with the directorates. In one site, a corporate savings plan was negotiated and divided by the number of directorates.

Cross-charging for radiology, pharmacy, dietetics and theatres was in operation on one site and for radiology and pharmacy on another. Standard costs or levels of re-charge were agreed between the relevant department and the directorate. Baseline activity levels were agreed, based on a rollover figure, and any known adjustments were made at pre-determined points throughout the year. However, service level agreements were not enforced. Directorates were responsible for the quantity of investigations; service departments were responsible for the price. In one site, pharmacy charges for services were based on a weighted workload, e.g. fifty items a year for the intensive care unit (ICU), and a multiplier was used for weighting. Using this system, the clinical director responsible for the pharmacy allocated hours to an individual service and pooled the remainder. The same site, however, moved towards a more detailed specification of allocations. At all sites there was no cross-charging for therapies but there were activity agreements in place. The advantage of cross-charging is that if the activity level goes up, it is a mechanism to cover variable costs. The disadvantages were mainly related to the amount of time required to produce costs and only the total direct costs were recharged, not overheads.

Directorates were in constant contact with their finance department. One site had an accountant based in the directorate. Others had a dedicated accountant, who worked with two or more directorates and was based in the finance department. The relationship was usually one of management support, in assisting the clinical management team to improve their ability to manage the budget.

Human Resources
Most sites had a liaison relationship with a central personnel department, with one site having devolved the personnel function, including the personnel staff, to individual clinical directorates. All the other sites considered it important to have a named person in the personnel department responsible for the personnel issues of the directorate. At some of the sites, it was suggested that basing the person in the clinical directorates resulted in de-professionalising the personnel function and the person involved lost touch with personnel affairs. The site that had devolved the personnel function ended up having to set up a central recruitment bureau because of duplication and inefficiencies.

The CEO was involved in the selection of clinical directors, in consultation with, and agreement from, consultant staff in the clinical directorate group. Two sites had a more formal selection process. In general, clinical directorates recruited their own staff, with the director of nursing being involved in the selection of senior nursing personnel. The central personnel department usually carried out the administrative role. Line managers in the clinical directorates recorded absenteeism manually. Individual performance appraisal was carried out in some clinical directorates across the interview sites, but not in all of them. Performance appraisal happened on a more consistent basis with nursing staff, and was usually based on objectives set between the manager and the appraised, with self-assessment, based on service developments, improvements and financial performance, being part of the process. It was used as a guide for training, development and career planning.

Succession planning was a problem in some of the sites, especially at clinical director level. In a clinical directorate on one site, the clinical director rotated every three months. Succession planning seemed a less obvious problem at nurse and business manager level, with the option of recruitment from other hospitals or identification of suitable people through individual performance appraisal being pursued. Three sites offered early retirement during the initial years of change. This option was made available to cope with the difficulty of involving older, senior staff in the change process. Chief executives and directors of nursing said that, for people who would not be able to operate in the new system, it was an important part of major organisational change. Out-placement or re-allocation of areas was also an option offered to some.

Communication

Good communication is central to the success of the clinical directorate system. Hospital council meetings and executive meetings were usually held twice a month, where corporate and directorate business was conducted, with activity and financial reports being discussed. One site had a senior sub-committee structure that included finance, quality management and human resources (HR). This structure was considered critical to conducting the hospital business. The committee reported to the trust board and the idea was the brainchild of the chairman, a private sector businessman.

Within directorates, management team meetings were usually held weekly, with the clinical director and the nurse and business managers, or directorate manager, attending. Directorate team meetings were usually held monthly, and were attended by the management team and all consultant staff. On one site, directorate managers met monthly to share ideas; a topic of interest was presented and discussed each month. At most sites, the director of nursing met nurse managers as a group every month to discuss development and quality initiatives. On one site, the director of nursing arranged half-away-days every month with the nurse managers and met senior nurses individually every six weeks.

These meetings were considered important to exchange ideas and identify and solve problems. Nurse managers and sisters met monthly.

Across the sites, clinical management teams devoted a lot of effort and time to communication within the team and between the team and the hospital executive. Despite this, communication was considered a real problem across the sites and many communications problems were unresolved. Senior middle managers communicated well, but information was not filtering through to professional groups. Nurse managers were isolated within directorates. There were no good informal support structures in place for them to assist each other and to discuss and share problems. While there was often good vertical communication, there was no horizontal communication. And it proved difficult to flow IT and other systems across an organisation.

A number of approaches were taken to respond to these communication deficits: one site commenced monthly operations management group meetings and monthly strategy meetings across directorates; two sites produced a newsletter; and one CEO undertook monthly information road shows.

Change Management

Overall responsibility for managing the change usually lay with a steering group, comprising consultants, the CEO or general manager, and the director of nursing. Some sites had a project manager and team responsible for the day-to-day running. Visits were made to established sites in the UK and the US to review structures and other operational practices. One site brought in a management consultant to assist in developing the directorate structure. The management consultant was brought in from another region and proceeded to implement the structure as it had prevailed in the region he came from. Initially, the structures were put in place using service managers only. As a result, the service managers were angry and refused to report to the clinical directors when they came into post. The medical consultants were suspicious, angry and did not cooperate. The CEO and medical consultants went to the US to look at alternative structures and develop a new proposal.

Two broad approaches were used to introduce the change. One could be described as the whole site or big bang approach, whereby, on a given day, the whole site moved over to the new system. The second could be described as the pilot initiative approach, involving a more cautious and incremental approach to the introduction of the change across the whole hospital. Among those interviewed, the most popular was the whole site approach, which was considered to be cleaner and more efficient. In the sites where the introduction was successful, the clinical directorate model was sold to the clinical directors as an empowerment exercise and usually involved a considerable amount of consultation with them before proceeding to implementation.

The director of nursing was central to facilitating the changing role of the nurse manager/senior nurse, with some nurse managers finding the change very difficult. Comments from the sites suggest that the nurse managers were disillusioned, unsupported and isolated in their new role. Historically, nurses had a strong power base in some of the sites and it was a fundamental cultural change for nurses to report to clinical directors. Some left, others took redundancy.

A single central decision-making group, either in the form of an executive group or hospital council, as the strategic policymaking body for the hospital as a whole, was usually put in place. This group comprised of the CEO, director of nursing/quality, medical director, director of finance, director of personnel, the facilities director, the director of corporate affairs and all clinical directors or group clinical directors. The sites considered this structure necessary to ensure development of a corporate strategy and a unifying framework for the clinical directorates.

Training and Development

This was the responsibility of individual clinical directorates and, where it was implemented, a multidisciplinary approach to courses was evident across the sites. Nurse managers and business managers were sent on courses, initially focusing on topics such as managing change, budget management, leadership, etc. One site concentrated training and development on the ward sisters, with total devolution of management authority and accountability being achieved. They were called ward managers. Line and senior management courses were available on three sites. Three sites encouraged away-days for staff within the directorates, to facilitate team building. Individual directorates held study days. Most sites bought in courses, such as customer care, interviewing and performance appraisal. Nurses tended to do best, with the director of nursing being responsible for training and development for nurses. Study days were organised for nurse managers and sisters. Development courses under the auspices of the King's Fund were held each year at a number of the sites.

One site had a central training and development department, responsible for training in-house people such as consultants, in areas such as budgeting, manpower planning, information systems and financial management. On all of the sites the IT departments ran courses on a regular basis. Budget holders for training and development included the director of nursing, the nurse managers, the business managers, and the HR and training and development departments.

Quality

This was a priority across the sites, with purchasers in the UK sites demanding quality at all levels as part of the contracting process, and often setting the quality agenda. At corporate level, quality was viewed as a continuous improvement process and was usually the responsibility of the director of nursing. At directorate level, initiatives were led by the nurse manager/senior nurse. At most sites, development officers, ranging in number from one to five and answerable to the director of nursing, had responsibility for liaising with the nurse manager/senior nurse in the clinical directorates in order to develop quality initiatives. Nursing initiatives included the nursing audit, the 'named nurse' policy and projects on issues such as pain, pressure sores and wound care and corporate initiatives such as quality standards relative to the patients' charter, and setting up a quality sub-committee chaired by the CEO, with assistance from the director of nursing. The director of nursing also handled patient satisfaction, feedback and complaints procedures.

The clinical director led medical audits in the clinical directorates. On most sites there was an audit department led by a medical director, with nurse and clerical assistants dedicated to specific directorates. Within the audit departments, work was usually carried out on approximately four topics per year, decided by the purchasers. Emphasis was on items in the patients' charter, such as waiting times. These items were singled out for particular attention because they were clearly measurable and had significant political importance and impact.

When interviewees were asked if they could identify any improvements in quality that stemmed directly from the introduction of the clinical directorate system, reference was usually made to improvements in internal services, in patient information systems and in patient accommodation.

Key Issues

A number of issues can be identified from the early stages of introducing resource management and clinical directorates, from the RM initiative in the UK, from the interim Brunel evaluation of that initiative, from the visits to the sites by the author and from the interviews conducted within St James's with those involved in the project. These issues are of particular importance to any change management initiative to avoid becoming too involved in organisational and managerial changes that do not necessarily affect outcomes. It is through the proper management of these issues that outcomes rather than arrangements will occupy centre stage as we further develop policy and practice in the area of clinical management. The issues can be summarised as:

- A strong sub-unit structure is important, with devolved budgetary responsibility.
- Senior hospital management must drive the change initiative and need to retain ownership of managing the change. The commitment of senior management to the management process should be manifested through lots of communication and sensitive management of the whole change process.
- Changing the culture is fundamental and it must happen throughout the organisation, with service providers involved in the planning and management of resources.
- Flexibility is essential in developing structures and, in particular, flexibility in the necessary modification of structures as they emerge. This includes the need for clarity in defining roles, combined with flexibility in how the roles develop.
- Information systems must be designed to support the work of the clinical directorates.
- It is important to recruit nurse managers and business managers with an appropriate level of experience and maturity. In particular, the nurse has an important role in clinical directorate structures in ensuring quality of patient care.
- Training and development is critical – and is usually underestimated – in progressing the organisation forward and in improving the ability of individuals to adapt to change.

- Those who may be marginalised through the provision of out-placement or early retirement arrangements should be handled with sensitivity.
- Effective communication is needed across the site. Problems can be anticipated and prevented by putting communication systems in place, such as meetings and sub-committee operational structures with the involvement of senior management.

Interviews with key personnel in St James's and in the hospitals surveyed showed that, in a period of change, one of the most difficult problems was that of communication. It was seen as an integral part of the management of the change process and was one of the most difficult to deal with.

The experience of St James's, in particular, provided one example of where a number of structures had been put in place to attempt to manage these issues. At strategic/policy level, a reorganisation project group was set up, comprising the CEO, deputy CEO/operations manager, director of nursing, six medical consultants and the management services manager. Its role includes policy and project framework/plan definition and development, and monitoring and controlling implementation of the project. Visits were made by members of the group to the UK and US to review structures and other operational practices. As indicated, at management level the deputy CEO/operations manager was responsible for implementation of the project. Centralised project support, to assist in the set-up process of all the directorates, was extended with the recruitment of a project manager responsible for planning and implementing the change project as defined. A project assistant supported the clinical directorates, assisting in all elements of the implementation of the plan. The hospital sites research showed the difficulties of communication across the whole hospital:

- There was no operational line between the directorates.
- The whole organisation was not looked at and issues affecting the whole organisation were not being dealt with.
- Communication within the hospital was a real problem; it was difficult to know what was going on in the rest of the hospital.

Managing an organisation in transition is probably one of the most difficult challenges facing any management team. This is particularly true when the organisation is a hospital, where the commitment and dedication of the individuals are crucial.

In the management of the change project within St James's and the other hospitals surveyed, therefore, senior management needed to be aware of where key individuals and key parts of the organisation were in this process. Clinical management requires the right kind of organisational structures within which to develop. It is not just about organisations; it is also about people. In implementing change it is important not to lose sight of the individuals: patients and service deliverers. This requires commitment and vision by the senior management teams involved in the process.

CHAPTER 4

Health Service Reform in Ireland

Shaping a Healthier Future

To put the development of clinical directorates in Ireland in context, we must review the evolution of Ireland's health service reform programme. Health policy was not a priority for Irish governments until the late 1940s, and public health services were delivered through the local government system. The Department of Local Government and Public Health looked after health issues. Influenced by public health developments in the UK, the Irish Government established a separate Department of Health in 1947. With the *Health Act, 1970*,[71] control of the health services was removed from the local authority system and re-organised as eight regional health boards under the ultimate control of the Department of Health. Each health board had a similar organisational structure, with the boards consisting of local authority councillors, representatives of the senior medical professions and nominees of the Minister for Health. The boards had three programme areas, each under a manager: hospital services, special or psychiatric hospitals, and community care. There were few health policy documents and those that were published tended to focus on organisational issues.[72]

The modern reform of the Irish health services can be said to have begun with the publication by the Department of Health in 1994 of an ambitious strategy, *Shaping a Healthier Future: A Strategy for Effective Healthcare in the 1990s*.[73] The strategy was based on three basic principles: equity, quality and accountability. On equity, the strategy proposed that access to health care should be determined by need for services, rather than ability to pay, and noted that, 'equity involves not only ensuring fairness but also being seen to be fair'.[74] On quality, it advocated a more modern approach, using techniques such as clinical audits, to ensure that the best possible outcome was achieved for the resources committed. Accountability was seen as requiring service providers to take responsibility for achieving agreed objectives and putting mechanisms in place to ensure that accountability is maximised.

The strategy was not produced in a vacuum. It was founded on the thinking contained in a number of earlier health policy documents. These included *Health: The Wider Dimensions* (1986),[75] a response to the World Health Organisation's programme, *Global Strategy for Health for All by the Year 2000* (1981);[76] the *Report of the Commission on Health Funding* (1989);[77] the Kennedy *Reports of the Dublin Hospitals Initiative Group* (1991);[78] the Hickey report on *Community Medicine and Public Health* (1990);[79] and others.

Quality and Fairness

In 2001, the Department of Health and Children published a new strategy, *Quality and Fairness: A Health System for You*,[80] which outlined a ten-year programme of investment and reform of the health system. It was built on the planned and strategic approach of the previous health strategy, as well as a number of other health-related strategies. It assessed progress over the previous seven years and took a fresh look at policy and objectives. It set clear priorities and involved all elements of the system. What distinguished the strategy was the unique level of consultation with individuals, professional groups, disciplines, voluntary organisations and state agencies on which it was based. It was the largest consultation process ever undertaken by the Government in the preparation of a strategy, with over 1,800 submissions considered. The new strategy set four overall national goals:

- Better health for everyone
- Fair access to publicly funded services
- Responsive and appropriate care delivery by an effective and efficient health system
- High performance in terms of quality of care, planning and decision-making, and accountability

The earlier strategy, *Shaping a Healthier Future*, was based on the three principles of equity, quality and accountability. *Quality and Fairness* added a fourth: people-centredness. This required that health and social services be delivered in a personalised way, in acknowledgement of individual service users' differences. Services were required to adapt to these differences in a number of ways, including accommodation of differences in patient/consumer preference, shared decision-making, provision of accessible, high quality information on health, and increased involvement of consumers as partners in planning and evaluation. Adapting to these services would require that:

- Services were to be organised, located and accessed in a way that took greater account of the needs and preferences of the community they served
- Health and social systems were able to accommodate differences in patient preference and encouraged shared decision-making
- Consumers were to be given greater control, but also greater responsibility, for their own health
- Consumers were to have access to high quality information on health to fully benefit from health and social systems and to participate in decisions relating to their health
- Increased involvement of consumers as partners in planning and evaluation would be an important component in promoting openness and accountability

The principle of equity recognised that health inequalities should be targeted and people treated fairly according to need. This principle was seen as central to developing policies to reduce the difference in health status across the social spectrum in Ireland and to ensure equitable access to services based on need. *Quality and Fairness* stated that access to health care should be fair and that the system must respond to people's needs – accessibility should not depend on geographic location or ability to pay.

A quality health system required evidence-based, externally validated standards (including guidelines and protocols) that were set in partnership with the consumers. Improving quality in the health system required implementation of these standards, ongoing education and commitment from health care institutions and professionals. A culture of quality in the system involved an interdisciplinary approach and continuous evaluation of the system by such means as audits and providing feedback to health care providers and consumers on the quality of care delivered and received. In addition to improving quality, evidence-based guidelines and tighter professional standards are aspects of accountability, which is underpinned in the formulation of the *Quality and Fairness* strategy.

The strategy proposed greater involvement by staff in planning and delivering services and a policy on staff participation to build on the partnership model. There would be renewed emphasis on the clinicians in management initiative, which is detailed in Chapter 8. Negotiation of the common contract for hospital consultants would be undertaken using a developmental agenda that would involve restructuring key elements of the current system to promote equity of access, organisation improvements and more clinical involvement in and responsibility for management programmes.

Frameworks for Change

Six areas were identified as the core frameworks for change:

- Reforming the acute hospital system
- Funding the health system
- Strengthening primary care
- Developing human resources
- Developing information
- Organisational reform

Each of these frameworks was the subject of a significant study aimed at introducing the necessary reforms:

- The *Report of the National Task Force on Medical Staffing* (the *Hanly Report*)[81] addressed the issues facing the acute hospital system.
- The *Report of the Commission on Financial Management and Control Systems in the Health Service* (the *Brennan Report*)[82] addressed the way in which the services are funded.
- *Primary Care: A New Direction,*[83] produced by the Department of Health and Children, addressed the issues facing primary care.
- *Action Plan for People Management,*[84] produced by the Department of Health and Children and the Health Service National Partnership, in consultation with the National Partnership Forum, responded to the key questions of human resource management.
- *Health Information: A National Strategy,*[85] produced by the Department of Health and Children, examined issues of information and quality within the services.
- The *Audit of Structures and Functions in the Health System,*[86] prepared by Prospectus Strategy Consultants (the *Prospectus*

Report), tackled the difficult and complex area of organisational reform.

The *Hanly Report*

The *Hanly Report* (2003) was the report of a task force charged with devising an implementation plan for reducing substantially the average working hours of non-consultant hospital doctors to meet the requirements of the European Working Time Directive (EWTD), to plan for the implementation of a consultant-provided service, and to address the associated medical education and training needs. This involved 'devising, costing and promoting implementation of a new model of hospital service delivery based on appropriately trained doctors providing patients with the highest quality service, using available resources as equitably, efficiently and effectively as possible'.[87]

The *Hanly Report* strongly supported the concept of involving health professionals, including medical, nursing and health and social care personnel, in key management decisions in acute hospitals and saw the clinical directorate model as one such example. It favoured systems that involved management, medical, nursing and other health professionals in a structured system, offering a genuine input to critical decisions of the hospital and encouraging cooperation between different specialties and disciplines: 'A vital requirement is to bring the management of and accountability for services to the "coalface" in a decentralised system of local decision-making.'[88] The report noted that a number of models of clinical directorate were already in place. That used in St James's Hospital, Dublin (see Chapter 3) had considerable advantages in the way in which it operated and the report saw a number of advantages in organising hospitals along the lines of clinical directorates or similar structures.

The *Hanly Report* believed that it was important to realise that no single clinical directorate model would be appropriate to all hospitals and that models appropriate to local needs, which involved health professionals and other staff in key decisions affecting the management of hospitals, should be developed and implemented. These models should include real devolution of budgetary responsibility for a designated unit or directorate within the hospital, with the relevant personnel trained to deal with the financial implications of devolved decision-making. Critical success factors would include:

- A system negotiated and agreed with all concerned
- A willingness by all health professionals and management to participate fully in the process and use it in the way intended; any model would fail quickly if some sought to bypass the need for this
- An explicit recognition of the need for reporting relationships that reflected the multidisciplinary nature of the team, rather than along traditional professional lines
- Well-developed information systems to support finance, staffing and activity requirements
- A carefully managed approach to implementation

The *Brennan Report*

The *Brennan Report* (2003) carried out a detailed examination and review of the financial management and control systems in the Irish health service. It found problems in the existing system and adopted four core principles in addressing these problems:

- The health service should be managed as a national system
- Accountability should rest with those who have the authority to commit the expenditure
- All costs incurred should be capable of being allocated to individual patients
- Good financial management and control should not be seen solely as a finance function

Recommendations in the report included:

- The establishment of an Executive to manage the Irish health service as a unitary national service
- A range of reforms of governance and financial management, control and reporting systems to support the Executive in the management of the system
- Substantial rationalisation of existing health agencies
- Strengthening the process of evaluation of clinical and cost-effectiveness for publicly funded drug schemes
- Pending the establishment of the Executive, the creation of a high level and well-resourced implementation committee

The *Brennan Report* noted that, to date in Ireland, the mechanisms that were central to effective clinical governance in the Irish health services had generally been patchy in their development. It recognised those who had worked in Ireland on individual initiatives that could play a role in the broader clinical governance agenda and identified that substantial progress had been made in involving clinicians in management and governance functions at a number of hospital sites, such as Cork University Hospital, St James's Hospital, and the Coombe Women's Hospital. But, the report cautioned, structural reform and improved information on the processes and effects of treatment would be of limited value unless they were underpinned by a coherent policy and legal framework.

It said that developing clinical governance mechanisms was demanding. It involved putting coordinated mechanisms in place to assess, assure and promote the quality of all aspects of clinical care. This would include quantitative and qualitative measures of care, assessment of variations in process, outcomes and access to care, rigorous risk management programmes and training in skills such as teamworking between caregivers. The report said that, while the clinicians in management initiative had attempted over a number of years to embrace some of this agenda, it was neither widespread nor elaborate enough. A whole-system approach was critically important and the current arrangements in relation to both GP services and hospital consultant services governed by the common contract were in need of review in order to ensure that accountability was as tight as it could be for all aspects of quality patient care. The areas that needed to be strengthened in a revised common contract for consultants included effective accountability for resources used, participation in managed clinical networks, flexible provision of clinical services and cooperation with clinical audits.

Primary Care: A New Direction

Primary Care: A New Direction (2001) was a document that complemented the main health strategy and signalled a shift of emphasis from over-reliance on acute services such as hospitals to one-stop-shops where patients could have access to GPs, nurses, physiotherapists, chiropodists, social workers and home helps.

The aims of the proposed developments were to provide 1) a strengthened primary care system that would play a more central role as the first and ongoing point of contact for people within the health care system; 2) an integrated, inter-disciplinary, high quality, team-based and user-friendly set of services for the public; and 3) enhanced capacity for primary care in the areas of disease prevention, rehabilitation and personal social services to complement the existing diagnosis and treatment focus.

71

The new system, to be implemented on a phased basis, would allow members of the general public to enrol with a team that included a GP. The teams would offer twenty-four-hour cover and, because of the number of different disciplines involved, they were designed to greatly reduce the demand for specialist services.

Action Plan for People Management

The *Action Plan for People Management* (2002) was developed by the Department of Health and Children and the Health Service Employers' Agency, in consultation with the National Partnership Forum. It addressed seven important themes identified in *Quality and Fairness*:

- Managing people effectively
- Improvements in the quality of working life
- Devising and implementing best practice employment policies and procedures
- Further development of the partnership approach in the health system
- Investment in training, development and education
- Promoting improved employee and industrial relations
- Development of performance management

Health Information: A National Strategy

Health Information: A National Strategy (2004) was a response to the need for greater health information by health care professionals and stakeholders, including patients, by ensuring that health information was more readily available and appropriately used throughout the sector. The strategy was driven by a consideration of the general health information needs of the stakeholders, who were faced with many barriers in finding relevant and reliable information. This was seen as largely due to the fragmented way in which information was being held and the under-use or availability of electronic systems. But the strategy focused on health information in its own right, rather than on information and communications technology.

Health professionals and other health service staff require a wide array of often complex information about their clients/patients to be immediately available. The information can be held in many different locations (laboratories, primary care files, hospital files) and reliance on the traditional paper record limits the extent to which care providers can share information in a useful, timely and seamless way.

The *Prospectus Report*

The primary objective of the *Prospectus Report* (2003) was to establish the organisational improvements needed to strengthen the capacity of the health system to meet the challenges of implementing the programme of development and reform set out in *Quality and Fairness*. Fifty-eight agencies were included in the audit. The key proposals for reform of the health system included:

- The creation of a consolidated health care structure
- Strengthening the functioning of the consolidated structure through the development of supporting processes
- Strengthening governance and accountability across the system
- Reorganisation of existing agencies and their functions in line with the consolidated structure

Health Service Reform Programme

The health service reform programme (HSRP),[89] announced in 2003, represented the most ambitious programme of change for the Irish health system in over thirty years. The programme was backed by a significant level of State investment: health expenditure in Ireland had increased from €3.7 billion in 1997 to almost €15 billion in 2008.[90]

The structural aspects of the HSRP emerged largely from the recommendations in the *Prospectus Report* and the *Brennan Report*. An information and consultation exercise was undertaken which directly reached over 20,000 staff working in the health system. The HSRP outlined a range of reforms to help deliver a more responsive, adaptable health system that would meet the needs of the population effectively and at an affordable cost. The programme was the implementation of key actions in relation to each of the six frameworks for change outlined in *Quality and Fairness*. It aimed to ensure that the health system was organised and managed in a way that would help it achieve the four national goals of the health strategy: better health for everyone, fair access, appropriate care in the appropriate setting and high performance.

The core theme of the HSRP has been the need to modernise health structures so they can deal with the demands placed on the system both currently and over the coming decades. Central to this is the ability to deliver a high quality of service for people on a consistent national basis. The reforms are designed to achieve a health service that provides high quality care, better value for money and improved health care management and the programme addresses a range of reforms to help modernise the health services to better meet the needs of patients.

The HSRP set out a range of structural, organisational, financial management and systems reforms aimed at delivering an improved health care delivery system in which consistent national, regional and local patient-centred care would be guaranteed; a better planned, managed and performance-measured system in which needs, services, funding and outputs were systematically interlinked; a health care system that maximised its use of resources by delivering the right care in the right setting; and making the Irish health services an employer of choice. Key elements of the programme were:

- Rationalising health service agencies to reduce fragmentation, including abolition of the health board/authority structures
- Establishing a Health Service Executive as a single national entity to manage health and personal social services
- Reorganising the Department of Health and Children, to enhance policy development and oversight
- Establishing a Health Information and Quality Authority (HIQA) to promote quality care throughout the health system
- Modernising supporting processes, such as service planning and management reporting to bring them in line with recognised international best practice
- Strengthening governance and accountability across the system

Health Service Executive

The *Health Act, 2004*[91] established the Health Service Executive (HSE), which came into operation in January 2005, with responsibility for the management and delivery of health and personal social services in the Republic of Ireland. According to the Act, the objective of the HSE is 'to use the resources available to it in the most beneficial, effective and efficient manner to improve, promote and protect the health and welfare of the public'.[92] The HSE was given responsibility for integrating the delivery of health and personal social services and it replaced the previous structure of ten regional health boards, the Eastern Regional Health Authority and a number of other agencies and organisations. The HSE is the largest organisation in the State, employing over 130,000 people.[93]

The HSE, as a single national entity, is intended to ensure that uniformly high quality safe services are provided across the system for the whole population and that a level playing pitch exists for statutory and non-statutory service providers in relation to the allocation of resources, the management of those resources and accountability for their use. In August 2005, Professor Brendan Drumm took up the post of chief executive officer. Significantly, the top manager in the Irish health services is a clinician.

The basis of the HSRP is the separation of policy formulation from service delivery. The creation of the HSE involved a complete separation of policy and executive functions and charged the Department of Health and Children with the role of monitoring and evaluating the work of the HSE and its expenditure. The HSE would, in turn, manage the health service as a single national entity and would also provide advice to the Minister and contribute to policy formulation. This approach was in line with the *Devlin Report* (1969),[94] which had a major influence on how the Government structured its operations, and which had recommended that Government Ministers should divest themselves of executive functions and focus on policy and planning.

The HSE's *Transformation Programme*

In December 2006, the HSE launched its *Transformation Programme 2007–2010*.[95] Aimed at the staff working for the HSE and related agencies (including voluntary hospitals and bodies), its vision is for everyone to have easy access to high quality care and services that they have confidence in and that staff are proud to provide.

In his introduction to the programme, Professor Drumm commented that the term 'reform' had become 'too closely associated with organisational and administrative change', whereas transformation was concerned with changing 'almost every aspect of our work [in the health and social care services]; the way we work, the way we relate to each other, our culture and our ambitions'.[96]

The programme set out six transformation priorities, which would be implemented through thirteen transformation programmes and associated projects. These programmes were categorised as those that would impact directly on services that patients, clients and carers receive and those aimed at improving the HSE's infrastructure and capability to provide and support these services.

The six transformation priorities were stated as follows:

- Many services are fragmented, disjointed and difficult to navigate. The priority is to develop integrated services across all stages of the care journey.
- There is inappropriate use and overreliance on acute hospital services. The priority is to configure primary, community and continuing care services so that they deliver optimal and cost-effective results.
- Accessing high quality acute hospital care can be difficult. The priority is to deliver optimal and cost-effective results.
- Inadequate and fragmented services for chronic illness are leading to unnecessary hospital admissions. The priority is to implement a model for the prevention and management of chronic illness.
- There is limited use of performance measurement. The priority is to implement standards-based performance measurement and management throughout the HSE.
- The work of staff can be frustrated by system and process constraints. The priority is to ensure all staff engage in transforming health and social care in Ireland.

The HSE's *Corporate Plan 2008–2011*[97] proposed to engage with staff and create work environments that support transformation. There would be more clinical involvement in the design and management of health and personal social services, with a move to a consultant-delivered rather than a consultant-led acute service, functioning within a well-developed clinical directorate structure. Clinical leadership and team-based service delivery would be embedded in the organisation.

The *Transformation Programme* recognised that the development of clinical directorates would represent a major step forward in the management and development of public health care in Ireland. In order to introduce clinical directorates and related systems of clinical leadership, achieving agreement on a new contractual framework for consultants was a key objective of the HSE. A new contract was agreed with medical unions in 2008 that included new management and organisational roles for clinical directors, with each consultant reporting to a clinical director.

For the longer term, the Minister for Health and Children, Mary Harney, TD, announced in 2009 the establishment of an Expert Group on Resource Allocation in the Health Sector,[98] chaired by Professor Frances Ruane, to examine how the existing system of resource allocation within the Irish public health service could be improved to support better the aims of the health reform programme: improved health status and outcomes for people; quality assurance and patient safety; speed and equity of access; and sustainability, within the resources provided. Minister Harney said[99] that the HSE had already begun work on ways of improving the efficiency and effectiveness of resource allocation and the Expert Group would be working with the HSE to find the most effective way to apply a given level of funding to achieve health policy goals.

The Minister went on to say:

> I want to see greatly improved links between resources and patients' interests. I want to make money follow the patient, that is, to support better each person's health status and outcomes from health care. The Group will be required to conduct its examination and formulate its recommendations on the basis of the existing amount of public funding for health. It is important to work within that budgetary context, because the more realistic the context, the more likely that recommendations can ultimately be implemented.[100]

The HSE's *Integrated Services Programme*

When the HSE was created, its principal service delivery arm was the health and personal social services division, which was initially divided into what were described as the three pillars of service delivery:

- **Population health**, which included functional units for health protection, health promotion, environmental health, emergency planning, strategic planning and evaluation, health intelligence, and transition and change.
- **Primary, community and continuing care (PCCC)**, was based on four geographically based units, each of which, in addition to the management of services within their area, has national responsibility for a different area of care. In addition, PCCC was responsible for local health offices, key elements in the management and development of services at a local level.
- **The national hospitals office (NHO)**, which was responsible for the management of the fifty-three hospitals throughout the country. In addition, the NHO was responsible for pre-hospital emergency care, including the ambulance service; contracts and utilisation; quality, risk and consumer affairs; and planning and development.

In July 2008, the HSE announced an *Integrated Services Programme*[101] that involved major organisation changes. The reorganisation was aimed at providing more local responsibility and authority within defined national parameters, more robust area structures and more clinical involvement in the design and management of health and social services, as well as accelerating the integration of primary, community and acute care. A new regional structure would have all services administered locally in specified geographical areas. Within the HSE, a new national director of quality and clinical care would drive clinical governance, quality and risk, define national clinical standards and protocols, and ensure engagement with clinical stakeholders. A single national directorate of integrated service delivery would have operational responsibility for all hospital- and community-based services. A national director of planning would lead integrated service planning. In effect, the three pillars would become two, with the population health pillar reassigned to the directorates and the elimination of the parallel systems for running hospital and community services.

As part of the *Integrated Services Programme*, and within the terms of the new contract, the HSE announced plans for the introduction of clinical directors throughout the health service on a two-year phased basis.[102] This is detailed in Chapters 6 and 7.

Among other objectives, the new structure was intended to provide clinical engagement at all levels and the facility for front-line clinicians and other professionals to make effective local decisions. Commenting on the proposals, Professor Drumm said that he could not overstate the importance of having clinicians (nurses, doctors, therapists, psychologists, social workers, etc.) involved in planning and managing care services at both national and regional level: 'When services have significant design and management leadership from clinicians they can deliver far better results.'[103] He said that the development of fully integrated health care – the essence of a modern health service – was the heart of the HSE's *Transformation Programme*. Central to all integrated health services were health professionals working in teams. This involved health professionals, regardless of whether they were hospital-based, community-based or both, actively sharing information, planning care and arranging tests and treatments that were delay-free and delivered the best value and convenience for patients and clients.

In May 2009, the HSE board approved new structures within which new regional directors would manage all services within four regional operating units, based on the existing administrative areas (Dublin Mid-Lenister; Dublin North-East; West; South). These units do not operate autonomously but within national policies, budgets, frameworks, and performance and safety standards. The board also confirmed that the NHO and PCCC directorates would become a single integrated services directorate.[104]

The global financial crisis in 2008, and its adverse impact on the Irish economy and on the scope for Government expenditure, has affected the pace of implementation of the continuing HSRP. Following the Supplementary Budget of April 2009, Minister Mary Harney affirmed that HSE faced a very difficult challenge but said that the economic and budgetary situation made it more, not less, important to continue to press ahead with the various reform initiatives that were already underway across all services: 'Revised ways of working, flexibility and innovation will be essential within the health services in order for patients to receive the continued provision of service levels they expect.'[105]

A similar point was made in her Department's *Statement of Strategy: 2008–2010*:

> In recent years the progress made by Ireland's economy has ensured that the resources available for public services, including health, increased significantly year on year. The short-term future now looks more uncertain, thus emphasising the importance of careful steward-ship of our resources, effective and appropriate prioritisation, and clear accountability.[106]

CHAPTER 5

Patient Safety and Patient-Centred Care

Building a Culture of Patient Safety

Building a Culture of Patient Safety, the report[107] of the Commission on Patient Safety and Quality Assurance, chaired by Dr Deirdre Madden, was published in 2008, largely in response to the findings of the *Lourdes Hospital Inquiry*[108] and to health system failures in other jurisdictions. The Commission was established in 2007, comprising representatives from medicine, nursing, management and patient groups, and was charged with developing proposals on patient safety and quality in health care. The Commission's report referred to incidents in Ireland relating to the misdiagnosis of cancer, 'which have highlighted yet again similar weaknesses and in particular also point strongly to poor management, governance and communications especially in circumstances where a serious adverse event takes place'.[109] The report commented: 'Public expectation of high performing services is legitimately developing and people are increasingly empowered to demand safe, high quality health care. As a result of these trends, improving the safety and assuring the quality of health care has emerged in recent years as a key challenge facing health systems internationally.'[110]

Patient safety has become a national and international imperative in recent years, with increased emphasis around the world on patient safety in policy reform, legislative changes and development of standards of care driven by quality improvement initiatives. Yet, despite a professionally trained and highly motivated workforce in the health system, and huge investment in health care services in recent years, the Irish health care system has lacked a framework aimed at reducing the likelihood of errors occurring and responding to errors. Nor has there been sufficient regulation in place to ensure as far as possible that patients receive the highest possible quality of care.

A number of high profile adverse events have resulted in inquiries and reports, which identified a range of safety-related issues, which were summarised in the Commission's report. These included weak governance structures, poor communication processes, failure to develop or implement clinical audits, poor working relations between clinicians and management, lack of senior clinical leadership within organisations and nationally, poor teamworking, lack of structured incident reporting systems, inconsistent analysis of adverse events, lack of clarity on reporting relationships and failure to participate in continuous professional development.

The Commission concluded that the shortcomings identified by these reports clearly pointed to the need for:

- Effective governance to ensure that the environment in which health care takes place would be supportive of safe and good quality care
- Greater accountability of institutions and their management for institutional performance
- Greater accountability in the different bodies that regulate clinical practice
- A strengthened system of information on adverse clinical events and complaints
- Patient reporting to be formalised, thereby providing a stronger role for patients and carers in feeding back on care received

The Commission put forward a vision or framework around which the Irish health system should be based: knowledgeable patients receiving safe and effective care from skilled professionals in appropriate environments with assessed outcomes. The values underpinning this framework would include openness, patient-centredness, learning, effectiveness and efficiency, good governance, leadership, evidence-based practice, accountability and patient/family involvement. 'Patients, carers and family members are and must be at the centre of all that is done in the Irish health service', the Commission said. 'Their voices must be heard more effectively in the future in relation to the development of policy for service delivery, development and evaluation.'[111]

The report said that good governance structures in health care should focus on patient safety in health care and noted that one structural suggestion to develop this focus was to organise clinicians into groups of patient-focused service configurations, commonly known as clinical streams or clinical directorates.

The publication of this report has significant implications for the implementation of clinical directorates in Ireland. It places patient safety and patient-centred care at the centre of the agenda for health service reform and for the development of the role of clinicians in management.

Health Information Technology

The *Building a Culture of Patient Safety* report said that it was essential in any health care system for its staff to be able to use information to monitor the safety and quality of the services being provided in order to facilitate the sharing of good practice, make improvements as required and inform service planning. Clinical effectiveness 'embraces this approach as part of a well governed health care system'.[112] Improvements in safety and quality in health care and the development of a high-reliability health care system cannot be contemplated without also considering the health information and health information technology (HIT) developments required to enable and sustain those improvements and extend the understanding and knowledge of the health system.

Health information technology is the use of information and communication technology in health care and may include:

- Electronic health records
- Personal health records
- E-mail communication
- Clinical alerts and reminders
- Computerised decision support systems
- Handheld devices
- Other technologies that store, protect, retrieve and transfer clinical, administrative and financial information stored electronically within health care settings

Practitioners need timely access to relevant information in order to deliver safe, high quality care. The *Building a Culture of Patient Safety* report pointed out, however, that access to information in health care is frequently limited or fragmented. Patient records were cited as being paper-based or, if computerised, available in formats that could not be shared easily between providers. Health service management information is usually collected for financial or administrative purposes rather than being directed at the outcomes of clinical care and the safety and quality of services. Clinical systems should be established and implemented with extensive clinical engagement and patient involvement in order to ensure that they capture comprehensive, meaningful, accurate and accessible information relating to every patient episode across the health system. Without such systems, it is impossible to assess the impact and outcomes of the care that is delivered to every patient and to the wider population.

The importance of health information and HIT to underpin the wider health reform programme has already been set out in a number of national strategy documents such as *Quality and Fairness*, the *Primary Care* strategy and the national health information strategy. Fit-for-purpose HIT, and therefore the necessary information and communication technology (ICT) systems, are essential to underpin a modern health system and to support the provision and accessibility of accurate and meaningful health information. HIT is commonly regarded as critical to the trans-formation of health care. However, the sector has lagged behind other sectors in the adoption of technology, and it is seen as a low priority, particularly when decisions to invest in ICT to improve patient safety are competing with other service delivery priorities. Delays in building these foundations often result in increasing costs and risks to the implementation of new information systems, when the existing legacy systems are out of date and are incompatible with new technology.

As part of the HSRP, the Department of Health and Children is preparing new legislation on the collection, use, sharing, storage, disclosure and transfer of personal health information as well as ensuring that the privacy of such information is appropriately respected. The main objectives of a new Health Information Bill[113] are to:

- Establish a legislative framework to enable information – in whatever form – to be used to best effect to enhance medical care and patient safety throughout the health system
- Facilitate the greater use of information technologies for better delivery of patient services
- Underpin an effective information governance structure for the health system generally

Health Information and Quality Authority

Health care provision in Ireland is continuously developing within a quality- and standards-driven agenda. The Health Information and Quality Authority (HIQA) was established in 2007 with the purpose of driving improvements in Ireland's health and social care services. It is responsible for quality and safety in Ireland's health and social care services through:

- Setting standards in health and social services
- Monitoring health care quality
- Social services inspectorate
- Health technology
- Health information

Reporting to the Minister for Health and Children, the role of the Authority is to 'promote safety and quality in the provision of health and personal social services for the benefit of the health and welfare of the public'.[114]

The HIQA set out its key objectives in its three-year *Corporate Plan 2008–2010*.[115] In this period, it aims to achieve the following:

- Build a capable and effective organisation that is well-governed and efficient
- Develop coherent person-centred standards to drive quality improvements across services, in line with identified priorities
- Monitor, investigate and, where necessary and appropriate, enforce quality and safety standards
- Provide a comprehensive information framework to support safe and efficient health and social care
- Undertake and support health technology assessments that inform investment decisions that are safe, effective and achieve value
- Report the findings of all work undertaken by the Authority and provide meaningful information about health and social care services to the general public, service users, health and social care professionals, policymakers and the Government
- Engage effectively with service users, service providers, policymakers and the Government to bring about sustainable improvements in our health and social care services

The Authority sets national standards for the provision of health and social care services (except for mental health services, which fall under the Mental Health Commission) in Ireland. These incorporate minimum standards for quality and safety for a given service, and developmental standards to support moving towards excellence, based on evidence and best practice within Ireland and internationally. The HIQA continuously monitors services to ensure that the standards are being met. Standards are monitored by multidisciplinary teams of professional and lay reviewers undertaking site visits and working with health care organisations to identify areas for improvement. The teams also recognise good practice. Quality assurance review reports are published on the Authority's website, together with an action plan from the service provider outlining a programme to address the recommendations of the report.

The HIQA is taking the lead in health technology assessment (HTA), many aspects of which are relatively new to Ireland and are being developed in line with national and international practice. Ireland has been one of the few developed countries with no systematic processes for evaluating the clinical and cost-effectiveness of its health services. In setting up Ireland's first HTA function, the HIQA is responsible for making sure that the resources in the health services are used in a way that ensures the best outcome for the patient or service user. This is done by assessing the clinical and cost-effectiveness of the medicines, devices, diagnostics and health promotion used across the health system. These assessments include the evaluation of social and ethical issues, quality of life and quality of end of life and cost-effectiveness in relation to health technology.

Health information is a critical part of the HIQA's work. As noted, the use of modern information technology (IT) in clinical care and administrative functions is helping to improve quality and safety of care for service users and support clinicians in delivering care. Better and faster information is the key to better decision-making and planning; a robust health information environment allows all stakeholders to make choices or decisions based on best available information. This is a fundamental requirement for a high-reliability health care system. The HIQA collaborates with key stakeholders on the development and implementation of electronic health records and a unique identifier for health and social care services in Ireland, which will mean faster referrals, fewer delays in ordering tests and reduced errors caused by handwriting.

HealthStat

An online hospital performance information and improvement system, HealthStat, was launched by the HSE in March 2009. Results are made available to the public. It uses a range of twenty-two indicators to give an overall picture of how services are being delivered under three headings: access, integration and resources. Access measures the waiting times that people experience for different services. Integration checks that the services received are patient-centred. Resources assess whether a hospital is making best use of its human and financial resources. Of the twenty-nine major hospitals rated in the first published assessment, most merited an 'average performance, room for improvement' rating. HealthStat will cover all general and speciality hospitals. A measurement of health and social care services provided by local health offices in the community will be provided from 2010.

Integrated Care Pathways

Integrated care pathways (ICPs) are structured multidisciplinary plans of care designed to support the implementation of clinical guidelines and protocols, such as clinical management, clinical and non-clinical resource management, clinical audits and also financial management.[116] They represent a continuum of care that identifies structures (institutions, facilities, etc.), care providers (clinical professionals) and processes (treatment paradigms) that intervene at critical points to efficiently treat the patient and achieve a defined outcome. Therefore, they provide detailed guidance for each stage in the management of a patient (assessment, intervention and treatment) with a specific condition over a given time period, and include progress and outcome details. In particular, ICPs aim to improve the continuity and coordination of care across different disciplines and sectors.

ICP development has enormous potential across every aspect of service delivery to contribute to driving and achieving the four national goals of the health strategy. Some of the principles that underpin the concept of ICP development, and thereby support national goals, are:

- Patient-centredness – ICPs focus on the individual patient, respecting the patient's choices, culture, social context and specific needs.

- Safety and quality – ICPs drive safety and quality by promoting evidence-based practice and factoring in continuous quality improvement at every point of health care delivery.
- Effectiveness – ICPs match care to science, identify ineffective care and provide the most reliable and up-to-date evidence to sustain effective health care.
- Timeliness – ICPs continually reduce waiting times and delays for both patients and those who provide health care.
- Efficiency – ICPs reduce inefficiency and thereby reduce waste and the total cost of health care; for example, waste of supplies, equipment, space, capital, ideas and human resources.
- Equity – ICPs, because they are patient-focused, provide opportunities to address and close socio-economic gaps in health status.

ICPs can be viewed as algorithms, inasmuch as they offer a flowchart format of the decisions to be made and the care to be provided for a given patient or patient group for a given condition in a systematic sequence. ICPs have four main components: a timeline; the categories of care or activities and their interventions; intermediate and long-term outcome criteria; and the variance record (to allow deviations to be documented and analysed). A number of activities may occur before or during the development of an integrated care pathway, including team member education and involvement, development of support systems, and standardisation.

The first step in developing an ICP is to map the patient's journey and the process involved in managing the clinical condition. Establishing a process map of the patient journey provides a structured approach and foundation to analyse care processes and service delivery from both a patient and service perspective. Therefore, in addition to providing an analysis of the patient journey, the process map can provide a clear picture of demand, activity and capacity.

Process mapping is a tool to capture the delivery of care at every stage of the patient journey. It focuses on care and service delivery from the patient's perspective and provides a detailed end-to-end view of the process and outcome of the patient's journey based on one person, one place, one time, regardless of whether the focus is on the patient condition group (e.g. asthma), procedure (e.g. knee replacement) or state or issue (e.g. falls in older people). Process mapping has the capability to identify the strengths and weaknesses in both the service and delivery of care, while also providing evidence supporting the need to review and develop solutions for change.

ICPs are designed to be dynamic multidisciplinary plans of care that alter in response to new evidence, demographic diversity, patient needs and system re-design. Monitoring and analysing variations from the ICP is a powerful tool to assist in ensuring quality of care and identifying patterns and trends that require further examination.

Clinical Practice Guidelines and Clinical Governance

Clinical practice guidelines are systematically developed statements to assist practitioners and consumer decisions about appropriate health care for specific clinical circumstances.[117] Irish health care organisations have embraced clinical practice guidelines to support appropriate and evidence-based care. Guidelines are a tool for consistency of care and may be seen as a way of closing the gap between what clinicians do and what scientific evidence supports.[118]

Good clinical guidelines aim to improve the quality of health care and clinical effectiveness. They can change the process of health care and improve people's chances of getting as well as possible. According to the National Institute for Health and Clinical Excellence, clinical guidelines can:

- Provide recommendations for the treatment and care of people by health professionals
- Be used to develop standards to assess the clinical practice of individual health professionals
- Be used in the education and training of health professionals
- Help patients to make informed decisions
- Improve communication between patients and health professionals[119]

The purpose of clinical practice guidelines is to identify effective diagnostic, screening and treatment strategies and encourage the use of these to improve the quality of health care and thus consumer outcomes. However, defining quality in health care can be difficult. One example of quality in health care is providing the right care, at the right time, for the right person, in the right way. Quality health care should be appropriate, accessible, effective, safe and provided by someone who is competent and accountable for practice.[120]

The *Building a Culture of Patient Safety* report detailed a review of international models of evidence-based practice (EBP) and asserted that supporting EBP was a critical element of a health system that aimed to deliver safe and high quality care and stated that clinical guidelines were a key intervention to support EBP and were often used in conjunction with ICPs and managed care. The report further stated that EBP is not a new concept in health care; its popularity has been augmented by suggestions that patients may have received care based on the unproven opinions of individual clinicians rather than on the evidence of their efficacy.[121] In EBP, the best methods of providing aspects of health care are identified and this knowledge is used to assist professionals in clinical decision-making. Evidence-based medicine is about integrating individual clinical expertise and the best external evidence; therefore, it is a conscientious, explicit and judicious use of current best evidence in making decisions about the care of individual patients. EBP may be best expressed as a component of an evidence-based health care approach that comprises three stages: producing evidence, making evidence available, and using evidence for decisions regarding individual patients (evidence-based clinical practice and evidence-based patient choice) or for populations or groups of patients (evidence-based public health and health service management).

Clinical governance is a framework through which health services organisations are accountable for continuously improving the quality of services and upholding high standards of clinical care to ensure patient safety. National recommendations and guidelines have the potential to promote equality of access for all and care based on the best available evidence. However, they also present challenges and potential conflict for nurses and for all clinical professionals in terms of accountability for decisions and actions in utilising clinical practice guidelines.[122] Accountability is a complex concept in health care and is recognised as a key driver for safety and quality of care. The key principles of good governance include having clear lines of accountability at individual, team and system level within an organisation.

The *Building a Culture of Patient Safety* report noted that, 'good governance structures in health care should focus on patient safety in health care. An example of one structural suggestion to develop this focus is to organise clinicians into groups of patient-focused service configurations, commonly known as clinical streams or clinical directorates.'[123] The Commission observed that, on the basis of international evidence, professionals should be accountable for their performance, not only to their professional bodies but also to the organisation in which they worked and ultimately to the patients and community they served. Clinicians needed to be integrated into senior management levels as this supported the desired culture. The Commission strongly supported the implementation of a system of clinical directorates within all health care organisations to ensure that the clinical director, appointed on a competency basis, would be accountable for all aspects of patient safety and quality within the directorate.

CHAPTER 6

The Establishment of
Clinical Directorates in Ireland

Launch of the Clinicians in Management Initiative

The health strategy *Quality and Fairness* (see Chapter 4) highlighted the key role of clinicians (doctors, nurses, and health and social care professionals) in the planning and delivery of a quality, patient-centred health service, particularly in relation to transparency and accountability. A central component of the role is to create and maintain effective working partnerships between clinicians and managers. This was the basis of the clinicians in management (CIM) initiative, which was launched by the Department of Health and Children in 1998 to strengthen the involvement of key health professionals in the planning and management of services.[124]

CIM was initially introduced in five pilot sites in Irish hospitals and, in 1999, there was a second wave rollout of CIM into seventeen additional hospitals, which was then further increased to thirty-one. Spearheading the initiative was the Office for Health Management (OHM), which had been set up in 1997 to implement the recommendations of the Department of Health and Children's management development strategy for the health and personal social services. To meet the needs of those involved in the implementation of the CIM agenda – individuals, teams and their organisations – the OHM gave support through the commissioning of skills development programmes, guidelines and discussion papers and acted as a facilitator for CIM project managers.

The OHM[125] noted that the CIM initiative complemented the HSRP in a number of respects. The reform programme recognised that clinician involvement was key to the continuous improvement of the health services and was concerned with involving clinicians in order to get better quality of care, better health outcomes and better value for money. Multidisciplinary teams could provide a much more seamless approach to the management of care than a highly divisionalised system. The *Hanly Report* explicitly acknowledged the value of consultant-provided services, in which a team of consultants works with junior doctors and other health professionals in multidisciplinary teams to deliver service directly to patients.

Role of the Clinician in Management

CIM was designed to provide a way to respond to and manage the rapid pace of change in the health care environment. As a result of new technological and clinical developments, it was now possible for services to support and treat a wider range of conditions than ever before. Public expectations of the health service – a wider range of services, delivered promptly and professionally – were constantly increasing. To meet these expectations and provide the range of services required, multi-professional teamworking was necessary. As a related factor, there was now increased scrutiny of the way in which health services were delivered, with a consequent need for clinical audits and clinical governance. Hard decisions had to be taken on resource allocation and prioritisation.[126]

In a series of discussion papers[127] prepared by the OHM, the CIM initiative was described as heralding the biggest change to the management of Irish hospitals for many years. It was designed with one primary objective: to improve the quality of care available to hospital patients. The aim of the initiative was to provide for balanced involvement in decision-making between doctors, nurses and allied health professionals, and to decentralise the responsibility for managing resources down to local units with their direct participation. It sought to build a sense of equal partnership between the various professional groups within the hospital, and give them a common focus on improving patient care. As previously noted, the term 'clinicians' encompasses all clinical professionals (doctors, nurses, psychologists, PAMs and other allied health care professionals) within an organisation.

In finding a way to involve clinicians in the management of health care facilities and services, a number of different models could be used and many different organisational structures were used in health care organisations throughout the world. No one structure was necessarily more advantageous than another; what was important was that the structure should meet the local requirements. However, the OHM discussion papers suggested that there were two basic principles: 1) creating a management board for the hospital, responsible for taking key corporate decisions on both short-term and long-term issues, and which had significant clinician involvement; and 2) devolving authority for the management of the business and the control of its resources to locally accountable units. Those organisations that lost sight of, or diluted, these fundamental principles typically ended up with cosmetic alterations to their management structures but a lack of real involvement by clinicians in the running of the hospital.

The benefits of CIM were summarised as:

- Improved patient care through better targeting of resources
- Greater opportunities to focus on quality initiatives
- Introduction of audits in clinical care, with consequent improvements
- Enhanced opportunities for professional development
- Better efficiency and reinvestment of resources into patient care
- Improved and better-defined relationships between managers and clinicians
- Better cross-disciplinary working and a better collective 'team spirit'
- More influence on top management of the organisation

In 2000, the OHM commissioned independent consultants to review the CIM initiative in the thirty-one hospitals throughout the country participating as second wave pilot sites. The principal conclusions of the report were that most hospitals viewed the initiative as a major change in the way hospitals were managed in Ireland. The imperative was to involve all senior staff, both managers and clinicians, at hospital level in determining priorities and in dealing with operational and planning issues. This was a culture change issue. However, the response had been largely in organisation structure.

The report, published in 2002,[128] concluded that this was not enough. Success would depend upon a greater focus on three factors. First, the process of introducing clinicians in management needed to be supported by a range of change management techniques, which, properly applied, would enable new structures and new roles to evolve. Second, the agenda that the teams at hospital level were expected to address needed to be balanced to include issues of central importance to the clinicians, such as clinical quality, governance and evidence-based practice. These issues have a natural professional focus for clinicians and, if they were adopted strategically at hospital level, they would enable doctors, nurses and health and social care professionals to exercise real leadership within their professional areas. Third, the skills and competencies of those involved in clinicians in management teams needed to be developed to enable them to work effectively in teams pursuing objectives in the context of overall hospital strategies.

The report said that the benefits of CIM should more clearly illustrate the positive impact upon patient care. Doctors from hospitals where the initiative was working very successfully could demonstrate the benefits. Hospitals could give the initiative more focus by allocating the bulk of a senior manager's time to leading and developing changes.

The review identified six stages of implementation:

- Exploration and consultation
- Investigation and information gathering
- Project planning
- Pilot implementation
- Full implementation
- Review and evaluation

The review noted that, while all pilot sites had embraced the initiative to some degree, most were still at the first three stages. Evidently, the most difficult step was to move from exploration, investigation and planning to actual implementation.

The review found some evidence of good multidisciplinary teamwork at several sites; but a number of issues emerged. Greater clarity was a key issue. There was a lack of consensus among professionals as to the purpose of the initiative and there was a need to re-state aims and objectives and emphasise that the focus was better patient care. There was also a need to clarify the role of doctors, nurses and especially the allied health professionals. Clarity was needed regarding the authority and responsibility for decision-making within hospitals, both for individuals and for clinical units. Some sites had become bogged down trying to create better organisational structures, which was less crucial to the outcome of better patient care than communication and consultation.

There were different levels of buy-in: Doctors were unclear about the boundaries of their decision-making and about the benefits of CIM. Directors of nursing and assistant directors of nursing were concerned about their changed roles. Unit nursing officers struggled with new relationships up and down the line. Nurses at mid-level were keen to move ahead. Allied health professionals were concerned about how they fitted into the new structure. The lack of sufficient formal performance measurement and scrutiny of practice made it difficult to measure the costs and benefits of changes in the delivery of health care. Implementing change impacts on resources, and a major difficulty in implementing CIM was the lack of financial or human resources to enable clinicians to devote more time to service management.

The review concluded:

> The Clinicians in Management initiative is about creating a partnership approach to replace a culture of professional rivalry where each profession and speciality guarded its own territory. This is a challenging task for any organisation. Whilst there is evidence of a considerable level of multidisciplinary work already taking place in our hospitals, there is much work to be done to achieve full partnership in the planning, management and delivery of health services. The change that is needed is not just a structural change but also a cultural change, a change which will empower professionals to work in partnership in delivering the best quality services within the resources available.[129]

OHM Leadership Survey

In 2002, the OHM published the results of a survey[130] that examined the views of hospital doctors in Ireland, their attitudes to participation in the leadership and management of their organisations and how leadership and management processes might best be facilitated. The survey showed unanimous support for clinical involvement in leadership at all levels, to ensure that the medical viewpoint was heard. Respondents recognised that their clinical practices had a major impact on both the quality and the quantity of service delivery and on resource allocation decisions. Most suggested that, regardless of the level of operation, the essence of clinical leadership lay in being proactive in seeking and influencing change, with colleagues and throughout the health system.

Respondents identified three levels of leadership: 1) across the organisation as a whole at corporate level ('influencing up'); 2) as head of a department or service ('influencing across'); and 3) as leader of one's own clinical team ('influencing down'). There was a common thread in the way effective clinical leaders approached the leadership task across these three levels of leadership. They used persuasion rather than hierarchical power to change peoples' attitudes and behaviour; produced evidence to back up their case to management and peers for change; provided examples of successful change to get colleagues on board; and prepared the ground in advance for major decisions through consultation and clarification with colleagues, anticipating possible problems in advance and providing options for action. The doctors interviewed were conscious that their credibility and acceptability among their peers rested on their ability to act as advocates for patient care and clinical service development, rather than as the clinical arm of executive management.

The motivation to become involved in clinical leadership stemmed mainly from professional values and vision for excellence in patient care, service delivery and working conditions. Some clinicians were spurred on by the climate for change in the health service. Others were of the opinion that those not involved early on might lose out later. Some reported getting involved in management roles in order to influence decisions regarding development of their own unit or department or directorate. Evidence of results – in other words demonstrable benefits to patients – was required to maintain clinicians' continuing commitment and motivation. There were also de-motivating factors, many stemming from shortcomings in organisational structures and functioning, or the absence of pre-existing effective working relationships with senior management. There was a widely shared sense of frustration with the decision-making and implementation processes in health care generally.

The research found that there was strong support for the principle of clinical leadership, and a very keen, shared motivator in the form of improvements to the quality of care. A number of critical success factors were identified:

- Commitment at both managerial and clinical levels
- The 'right' person for the job of clinical leader
- Clear roles and responsibilities for clinical leaders and managers
- Objective evidence of success
- Structures and decision-making processes to support and facilitate shared decision-making
- Access to support functions, for example, finance and information systems

- Adequate time and compensation for clinicians taking on the job
- Organisation development to facilitate change, and training and development to enhance personal capacity

In 2004, the OHM's newsletter reported that, though notable progress in introducing and implementing CIM had been made in a number of hospitals, countrywide, the experience had been variable: 'Five years on from the launch of CIM, full clinician involvement in decision-making and in the management of resources is not yet the norm across the health service.'[131]

The *Buttimer Report*

The report of the postgraduate medical education and training group chaired by Dr Jane Buttimer, *Preparing Ireland's Doctors to Meet the Health Needs of the 21st Century*,[132] and published in 2006 commented that the changing environment in which doctors would be delivering their services would include clinicians integrated into the managerial process, in clinical governance systems including a consultant team-provided service, better use of technology and consultants delivering training as well as continuing training in a more structured manner. It said that doctors would have to begin to hone the necessary skills early in their training and continue developing them throughout their careers:

> Because clinicians are at the core of both clinical work and education and training, they should be at the heart of clinical governance. Recognition of this fact, by clinicians, managers and policy-makers, is central to establishing responsible autonomy in medical education and training. To be effective, clinical governance should reach every level of the health care organisation. Structures and processes should be put in place in ways that will engage clinicians and generate improvements in medical education and training.[133]

The report recommended that the CIM initiative should be extended to all hospital sites. It urged that HSE medical education, training and research (HSE-METR) and the relevant policy sections of the Department of Health and Children should examine at an early stage the scope for involving consultant trainers in the management of medical education and training in line with CIM.

Comptroller and Auditor General's Report

In March 2007, the Comptroller and Auditor General issued a special report: *Medical Consultants' Contract*.[134] It found that nearly all the acute hospitals had full executive management boards or similar structures in place with varying degrees of consultant involvement. However, at the unit grouping level, more refinement was needed in most cases before the arrangements could be regarded as effective clinical directorates. Regarding CIM, the report found that, while considerable management change had taken place since 1997, the pace of change had not been as fast as might reasonably be expected in a ten-year time frame.

The report noted that the overall aim of clinical directorates was to have mechanisms in place which ensured that consultants and hospital managers worked together within agreed structures and dealt with shared agendas, such as hospital quality assurance, clinical audits, performance outcome, strategy development and service planning. It found that these sub-board structures existed, at least to some extent, in thirty-nine hospitals. Some hospitals were taking steps to move in that direction – for instance, Beaumont and Tallaght had indicated that they intended to move towards a clinical directorate model from other centralised and hybrid structures. Eight other hospitals indicated that only some sub-board structures were in place or in development. Twelve indicated that no sub-board structures were set up to facilitate participation of consultants in the management process.

The *Comptroller and Auditor General's Report* said that individual hospitals had different models to facilitate participation of consultants in hospital management, but their involvement was generally in the areas of clinical standards and clinical audits and not in budget control, resource planning, strategy development or operations management. To the extent that involvement had been achieved in some cases, it took place within a voluntary system with no specific incentive or compulsion to participate. In order to guide change at local level, national standards and norms were essential. Without standards and a mandate from the HSE to implement appropriate structures, hospitals continued to operate in accordance with local arrangements. Short of formal arrangements, the report found good examples of consultants and management working together to manage their hospital and services. For example, the report's examination team was informed by Roscommon County

Hospital that they had no 'clinicians in management' model in operation within the hospital. Yet, all ten of their consultants were part of the hospital management team. When the hospital had recently underwent a capital refurbishment programme, all consultants worked with hospital management to change their sessions to meet and support the hospital service needs. This, said the report, was an example of cooperation between consultants and management to the benefit of patient care.

The report concluded that consultants were involved to a greater or lesser extent in management. But there was little consistency from hospital to hospital in the scope of their involvement. There appeared to be a need to clearly define the objectives and structures of a clinical directorate model. According to the report, 'at a minimum it might include day-to-day responsibility for services, resource utilisation and a framework for monitoring the quality of outputs subject to overall accountability to hospital management'.[135] There was a divide between accountability for allocation and application of resources on the one hand and responsibility for service outcomes on the other. Budgetary decisions were reserved for management while service outcomes were primarily the responsibility of consultants. The report recognised that increased involvement of consultants in resource allocation and resource rationing gave rise to a need to reconcile their obligations to patients with the reality that resources were finite: 'However, the moral imperative to do the best for patients while arguing for better resource allocation and application can also be seen as an argument for greater involvement.'[136]

The HSE and Clinical Directorates

In its *National Service Plan 2006*,[137] the HSE said that it would develop models of teamworking, including further development of CIM, to contribute to enhanced teamworking and service delivery, with models for each service developed and implementation plans agreed. CIM became closely aligned with the concept of clinical directorates and the clinical directorate concept became the explicit HSE instrument for directly involving clinicians in the management of a hospital or operational area. The HSE *Corporate Plan 2008–2011*[138] said that services would move to a consultant-delivered rather than a consultant-led acute service, functioning within a well-developed clinical directorate structure.

The corporate plan announced the introduction of a new integrated clinical and corporate governance structure to support the concept of integrated working practices and clinical networks. Clinical leadership and team-based service delivery would be embedded in the organisation:

> Health professionals will have a greater input in the planning and management of health services as individuals, in teams and in their organisation, with the primary purpose of providing better quality patient care, and hospitals will have management arrangements, structures and processes to take full advantage of the opportunities in line with the implementation of the Clinicians in Management Initiative.[139]

The HSE agreed a new contract with the Irish Medical Organisation and the Irish Hospital Consultants Association in 2008 that included provision for the introduction of clinical directorates. The contract recognised the importance of the role of clinical director, which placed consultants within the leadership structure in the management of the health service. The contract came into effect in January 2009.[140]

The contract specified that the consultant would generally work as part of a consultant team, whose primary purpose was to ensure consultant-provided services to patients on a frequent and continuing basis. This would require the consultant to provide diagnosis, treatment and care to patients under the care of other consultants on the consultant team and vice versa. Membership of the consultant team would be determined in the context of the local working environment and the team might be defined at specialty/sub-speciality level or under a more broadly based categorisation, such as general medicine or general surgery. The consultant would participate in the development and operation of the clinical directorate structure and in other existing or future management or representative structures, and would receive training and support to enable him or her to participate.

The contract provided a template for a directorate service plan, which specified the available resources and funding and how these would be deployed in delivering services. The consultant was described as simultaneously the key directorate resource with respect to service delivery and the core decision-maker regarding utilisation of the resources of the directorate and the organisation.

The clinical director would be responsible for developing and implementing the service plan, with the participation of directorate personnel. The service plan would quantify the total resources available to the directorate; specify services to be delivered through these resources; determine how to deploy resources in a manner that would optimise service delivery in the context of the requirements of the corporate service plan; and determine assignments and work schedules for consultants.

The responsibilities of the clinical director indicated the degree to which management was devolved to the directorates. In addition to preparing and managing the service plan, the clinical director's responsibilities covered:

- Providing strategic input and clinical advice
- Monitoring and controlling directorate performance against planned clinical, business and budgetary performance indicators
- Identifying service development priorities and annual budget bids
- Implementing clinical audits
- Developing practice plans with individual consultants and monitoring their implementation
- Fostering teamworking
- Implementing the measures required to meet accreditation requirements
- Implementing and complying with risk management policy and provisions
- Participating in the grievance and disciplinary procedures in line with corporate policy
- Ensuring a consistency of approach in the application of corporate and ethical standards and clinical protocols in accordance with best practice
- Contributing to effective communications within the directorate, across the hospital or service and with external stakeholders
- Supporting clinical training and continuing professional development
- Fostering a culture of teaching and research within the directorate
- Participating in the recruitment of permanent, temporary and locum staff as required
- Engaging with service users and representatives to include their perspective in service management

In a briefing document announcing the appointment of clinical directors – *Clinical Directorates: The Way Forward*[141] – issued in

August 2008, the HSE said that clinical directorates were central to its commitment to having consultants function as senior clinical leaders and decision-makers in the public health service. The HSE said that feedback from clinicians, network managers, local health managers and hospital managers would shape the HSE's approach in a number of areas. These included the need to see this role as a leadership role, in addition to the operational role as outlined in the contract, and fully acknowledging the leadership role of the clinical director as a core element rather than an add-on to clinical practice. Directorates would focus on specific tasks that would improve the patient experience and directors would be empowered and provided with significant management resources approved to support them. An agreed management approach at network/ hospital level would ensure that this role could be fully executed.

Professor Drumm said that the HSE was committed to enabling consultants to function as senior clinical leaders and decision-makers in the public health service, and clinical directors were central to this new way forward. He said, 'We have for the first time the prospect of significantly empowering clinicians as the key designers and leaders of modern health services at all levels right across the organisation. We know from experience that when care services have significant leadership from clinicians they deliver far better results in terms of clinical effectiveness, patient safety, patient outcomes and financial returns.' He announced that, beginning immediately, and continuing over the next two years, clinical directorates would evolve on a staged basis with responsibilities gradually devolved to clinical directors.[142]

The HSE sees the primary role of a clinical director as one of deploying and managing consultants and other resources, planning how services are delivered and contributing to the process of strategic planning, as well as influencing and responding to organisational priorities. This involves responsibility for agreeing an annual directorate service plan, identifying service development priorities and aligning directorate service plans with hospital or network plans. A clinical director might cover one speciality area or a range of specialities. A clinical director, generally supported by a nurse manager and a business manager, would head each directorate.[143]

Professor Drumm said that a priority was to ensure that clinical directorates operated consistently, in accordance with international best practice, and delivered for patients and clients a modern, high quality and easily accessible service. 'Clinical directorates can unlock our potential to transform and modernise all patient and client services, hospital-based and community-based', he said. 'They represent a major step forward in reorienting our public health service.'[144] The briefing document stated that the directorates would be responsible for how patient and client services were developed and delivered to defined populations across care groups, service settings and professional disciplines. Clinical directorates must be large enough to justify comprehensive support by business managers, thereby empowering them to drive change. This would require existing management resources, budgetary allocation, financial reporting systems and other corporate and business functions to be adjusted. In practice, this would mean that clinical directorates would be based on a minimum of thirty to sixty whole-time consultant posts.[145]

The HSE has developed guiding principles and criteria.[146] Clinical directors and their directorates will:

- Focus on the provision of safe, efficient and patient-centred services
- Be configured in a way that will allow them to address the needs of patients and clients from the service entry point to the exit point
- Be responsible for all the clinical services that are needed for a typical patient/client journey
- Transcend hospital–community boundaries and be based on patient journeys and care pathways
- Be led by senior clinicians, nominated by consultants
- Be large enough to be empowered to lead and shape change

Clinical directors will:

- Be senior clinical leaders – with defined organisational and clinical responsibilities
- Have senior executive support
- Be supported by leadership and corporate development programmes to strengthen their capabilities as required
- Enjoy the confidence of their colleagues as leaders while, at the same time, have the ability to be objective in the area of performance management and measurement
- Be recognised as leaders by their colleagues, employers and the HSE

Clinical directorates will evolve on a staged basis. As an initial step, one clinical director is appointed in each hospital group within the acute system. Medium-sized hospitals, with thirty to sixty whole-time consultant posts, will have a single clinical director. In larger hospitals, with more than sixty to seventy whole-time consultant posts, there will ultimately be two to four 'core' clinical directorates. The development of clinical directorates and the appointment of clinical directors are seen as a critical work stream within the overall HSE *Transformation Programme*. Clinical directorates will expand over time to encompass service delivery across the social care and personal social services programmes. This will include a wide range of social care and personal social services, such as services for people with disabilities or social inclusion services targeted at supporting disadvantaged people. Over one hundred clinical directors are planned. The first forty appointments were made in January 2009.[147]

CHAPTER 7

Governance and Clinical Directorates in Ireland

Principles and Framework

In June 2009, the HSE produced guidelines for the creation of clinical directorates, entitled *Clinical Directorates: Principles and Framework*.[148] The document was intended to outline a national principles-based framework within which all clinical directorates should be implemented (with the exception of mental health – see separate section in this chapter on clinical directorates and mental health). While there should be scope for adaptation to meet local needs, the document established the principle that all clinical directorates should fit within this national framework. It is important to remember that the experience of implementing clinical directorates elsewhere (see Chapters 1, 2 and 3) would indicate that this is a dynamic process subject to change. It is likely, therefore, that there will be amendments to the principles and framework provided as the experience of implementation grows.

The HSE describes the purpose of clinical directorates as being to achieve the best clinical outcomes and experience for patients within the available resources. The viability of the directorates is seen as dependent on the involvement of clinicians, understood in this context as medical consultants, in leadership positions as clinical directors with executive authority, working in a collaborative manner with other key staff, including management, nursing and health and social care professions. It is recognised that this is one of the most significant changes to occur in the Irish health care service for many years and presents an unprecedented opportunity for change through clinical leadership.

It represents an explicit recognition of the fact that clinical directors in Ireland will, in all cases, be medical consultants. This is a principle that emanates logically from the new consultant contract, which required all consultants to report to a clinical director and play a full role in the management of clinical services.[149]

The document should be read in conjunction with the guidelines on clinical leadership[150] (dealt with later in this chapter), which make it clear that, while the clinical director provides clinical and executive leadership within the directorate, all clinical professionals have a duty to provide leadership in their own specific areas of competence as part of multidisciplinary teams.

Each clinical director will take the lead in the development of a local clinical directorate model, appropriate to the particular local or regional circumstances, in accordance with the national *Principles and Framework*. In doing this, the clinical director must work in close collaboration with the hospital manager or CEO, and the regional and national clinical directorate structures, including the office of the national director of quality and clinical care. All proposed directorate models are subject to review, assessment and approval by a HSE/forum review group prior to implementation. Subsequent modifications, in response to changing circumstances and the changing needs of the service, are also to be approved by this review group. The group will review the general operation and performance of the clinical directorate annually to assess its performance against stated objectives. The process and methodology of this review would be defined before the end of 2009 with input from stakeholders.

Regarding the scope and structure of clinical directorates, the framework states that, in determining the optimum clinical directorate model in any particular situation, factors to be considered include population served; care pathways; existing or planned service configuration within the institution, network or region; and workload. Clinical directorates must put forward the supporting rationale for their proposed model. Directorates cannot be confined to a single specialty – they must be grouped in logical units that reflect a patient's care pathway within the institution, groups of institutions or networks, and to and from the community. Possible options for the configuration of directorates include perioperative, medical, women and children's health, and mental health.

An institution might have one or more directorates. A single directorate could cover more than one institution or entity; possibly a national directorate for a particular specialty. Interfaces between directorates must be explicit, for example, general hospital referring to tertiary hospital or centre. Depending on local circumstances, it may be appropriate for some institutions to form part of a larger directorate model, rather than being stand alone; however, proposed clinical directorates must give specific attention to linkages across the spectrum of primary, community and continuing care.

Each clinical directorate model should outline the substructures required to enable their effective operation, in line with evolving national and regional clinical and managerial governance structures. These substructures, for example, could include specialty, departmental or site clinical leads. Equally, consideration should be given to situations where, for example, a number of connected clinical directorates may have an overall lead clinical director. This model should demonstrate how resources would be fairly and appropriately allocated across related directorates. Proposed clinical directorates must give specific attention to ensure linkages across the spectrum of hospital, primary, community and continuing care, as the integrated model of service delivery develops over time. Clinical directorates should also formalise clinical interfaces with other directorates, primary care and community care as deemed appropriate. This will be required where patients need to access services in more than one directorate, e.g. a psychiatric patient requiring acute medical service.

Table 1 provides examples of the kinds of linkages that a clinical director in a specific clinical directorate should develop with primary care teams (PCTs) in the community.

The framework also makes it clear that a clinical directorate must be sufficient in scale to have a significant impact on the quality and safety of patient care, but not so large as to become ineffective. In the initial phases, it is important that each clinical directorate

Table 1: Examples of Linkages between Clinical Directorates and the Community

Clinical Directorate	The Clinical Director Will Need to Develop Linkages with PCTs in Areas such as:
Medicine	Discharge planning Agreed formularies for drug prescribing Chronic disease management IV therapy in the community Shared care for inpatient treatment episodes Assessment for aids and appliances Diabetes, COPD, stroke, etc. protocols Community intervention teams

(Continued)

Table 1: (Continued)

Clinical Directorate	The Clinical Director Will Need to Develop Linkages with PCTs in Areas such as:
Surgery	Direct access surgery Minor injuries in primary care and A&E Minor surgery Brain acquired injury Wound care
Diagnostics	Protocols for laboratory/radiology services Access for PCTs Liaison regarding appropriate testing, e.g. headache and MRI/CT scan Point of care testing
Obstetrics	Domino deliveries Pre- and post-natal care Shared antenatal care
Cancer	Referral/discharge guidelines – agreed protocols Discharge following treatment Shared care GP minor surgery protocols Palliative care
Mental health	Child and adolescent mental health services Shared care for inpatient treatment episodes Eating disorders Old age psychiatry Crisis response service Forensic services PCTs
Children and families	Child development screening Child protection Immunisation Therapy supports, e.g. speech and language, audiology, PCTs
Disabilities	Agreed protocols on chronic illness, e.g. ABI Early intervention services Integration with PCT therapies Rehabilitation in the community PCTs
Social inclusion	Hepatitis B Addiction services, e.g. alcohol Travellers/ethnic minorities Homeless services PCTs

(Continued)

Table 1: (Continued)

Clinical Directorate	The Clinical Director Will Need to Develop Linkages with PCTs in Areas such as:
Older persons	Community intervention teams
	IV in residential settings
	Maintaining older persons in the community
	Rapid access clinics
	Home care packages
	Continence services
	Elder abuse
	Community geriatricians
	PCTs

Source: HSE (2009a: 8), © HSE, 2009, reproduced with permission.

focuses on a number of priority areas and processes (such as discharge planning and waiting lists) and works to utilise the resources of the directorate in these areas. Such priorities should refer to a national set of priorities to be defined through the directorate of clinical care and quality (described in more detail later in this chapter).

The clinical director must be in a position to allocate a meaningful time commitment to the role – defined as a minimum of 50 per cent of the clinical director's time and reviewed on an ongoing basis. It is the responsibility of the network manager, in collaboration with the clinical director and the local manager, to re-allocate resources to meet this requirement.

The framework also makes reference to the importance of understanding the transitional nature of the role to be adopted by the initial cohort of clinical directors. In most instances, these first clinical directors will be engaged in activities related to the definition and establishment of a clinical directorate model within their sphere of operation. During this transitional phase, it is critical that the clinical director and hospital manager/CEO work very closely together in order to devise the optimum directorate model. In the future, the clinical director will mainly be concerned with the leadership and management of an operational directorate.

While the clinical director will have a strong management function in the clinical directorate, the leadership role is equally, if not more, important. In the management role, the clinical director will be involved in planning, budgeting, organising, staffing and problem-solving. In the leadership role, the clinical director will be responsible for setting direction, aligning and motivating people, and producing change, ultimately developing a culture of 'common purpose' with everyone striving for the same goal irrespective of role.

The clinical director should report to the relevant hospital manager/CEO. In some situations, there may be a need to establish a lead clinical director, particularly where the sphere of operations is exceptionally broad and complex, requiring multiple directorates. In such circumstances a clinical director may report to a lead clinical director. The clinical director will have a direct link to the regional clinical director and to the national director of clinical care and quality on clinical and quality issues.

The role of the clinical director is dependent on the exercise of authority, both moral and actual. Moral authority will derive from the leadership characteristics of the individual clinical director, i.e. perceived capability, professional respect, trust, communication skills, ability to build relationships, quality of decision-making, etc. The loss of moral authority will seriously, and potentially fatally, undermine the ability of the clinical director to fulfil the role. Actual authority derives from the contractual nature of the role, and the influence the clinical director can bring to bear on the allocation of resources within the directorate. Clinical directorates should be responsible and accountable for the allocation of funding and resources to its defined priorities, which, in the initial stage of implementation, are likely to be the areas of performance and clinical risk and safety in line with the HSE quality, safety and risk framework.

The clinical directors should establish a close and effective core team and working relationship between the clinical director, the CEO/hospital manager, the director of nursing, and health and social care professionals. Clinical directorates should recognise the relationship of interdependence and co-leadership between clinical directors and hospital management. The principle of mutual respect and trust must be embedded in the organisational culture. Communication, particularly face to face, will be critically important. The clinical directorate must have a physical presence (e.g. office, email address) within the institution – it should not be a 'virtual' entity – and should have appropriate support (business manager, secretarial).

The framework also provided a template for the preparation of proposals for submission to the HSE/forum review group. The principles outlined above provide the basis on which individual proposals will be assessed. In preparing these submissions, information should be presented in relation to the aims and objectives of the clinical directorate, the governance structure, the clinical business plan, education and training, support, and the management of data. Submissions should clearly state their purpose. The purpose should be underpinned by clear objectives and deliverables. Care should be taken to ensure that the 'patient journey' is at the centre – a core objective of the directorate model is to meet the clinical needs of patients in the most logical and effective manner. Objectives should be concrete, time-limited and achievable. They should be linked to national objectives where these are available.

Each clinical directorate should also outline its governance structure. Where more than one directorate is proposed within an institution or network, there must be an explicit statement regarding the interface and interdependence between them. Among other things, this should address the roles and linkages between the national directorates and the clinical director, the clinical director and CEO/hospital manager, the director of nursing, health and social care professionals, the medical board, clinical leads and departments, the finance director, regional clinical directors, network managers, other directorates both within and outside the institution, and other committees of the institution. For voluntary hospitals, the relationship between the hospital board, clinical directorates, CEOs and medical boards should be stated. Appropriate supporting sub-systems and superstructures must be identified. A core principle is that the clinical directorate should be inclusive, and that all stakeholders must feel that they are integral to it. At the same time, decision-making must be sensible, evidence-based and clear-cut, i.e. decisions must be made, and cannot depend on total consensus. Clear statements should be made as regards the issue of responsibility and accountability. Reporting structures should be stated.

Based on the objectives, a three-year clinical business plan should be developed. This plan, in line with the HSE corporate plan and national service plan, should outline how the objectives are to be achieved. Issues to be addressed in the plan include timelines and milestones; reporting; performance measurement and management; standards to be achieved in line with the HSE's quality, safety and risk framework; contingency, i.e. if certain elements of the plan are not achieved, or if inputs change; and resources, including personnel, financial and physical, and their allocation.

On education and training, high quality professional staff, working in a well-structured and effective environment, have a hugely important effect on the quality of care experienced by the patient. The clinical directorate should set out its approach to supporting undergraduate and postgraduate education and training and continuous professional development within the context of the clinical business plan. This is particularly important given the fact that postgraduate medical trainees are deeply involved in all aspects of service and the need for specialists to meet competence assurance requirements through audits, multi-source feedback and continuous professional development.

The directorate should state the support to be provided to the functioning of the directorate, including the clinical director. This should include office accommodation, administrative support, local facilitation, a clinical director network and formal linkages with regional clinical directors. Clinical directors should avail of peer support arrangements.

Finally, according to the template, an essential input to the clinical directorate in terms of effective decision-making is the availability of valid, timely and reliable data. The directorate should establish the elements of data required for its effective functioning and outline the methodologies and protocols relating to the production of such data.

Clinical Leadership

In addition to the *Principles and Framework* document, the HSE also produced in May 2009 a discussion paper entitled *Achieving Excellence in Clinical Governance: A Distributed Clinical Leadership Model for the HSE – Ensuring the Health and Personal Social Care System Is in Good Hands*.[151] This discussion paper provides an initial attempt at defining a model for distributed clinical leadership within the HSE. As with other guidance documents provided at the early stage of the implementation of clinical directorates, it is highly likely that the content of this paper will be subject to change as experience grows. The paper recognises the growing importance being given in international health service circles to the development of frameworks that emphasise the importance of clinical leadership throughout the system.

Mountford and Webb,[152] writing in the *McKinsey Quarterly* in February 2009, state:

A growing body of research supports the assertion that effective clinical leadership lifts the performance of health care organisations. A recent study by McKinsey and the London School of Economics, for example, found that hospitals with the greatest clinician participation in management scored about 50 percent higher on important drivers of performance than hospitals with low levels of clinical leadership did. In the United States and elsewhere, academic studies report that high-performing medical groups typically emphasise clinical quality, build deep relationships between clinicians and non-clinicians, and are quick to learn new ways of working. A recent study by the UK National Health Service found that, in eleven cases of attempted improvement in services, organisations with stronger clinical leadership were more successful, while another UK study found that CEOs in the highest-performing organisations engaged clinicians in dialogue and in joint problem-solving efforts.

The Ministerial Task Group on clinical leadership in New Zealand is clear about the benefits to the health care system of good clinical leadership: 'Health care that has competent, diffuse, transformational, shared leadership is safe, effective, resource-efficient and economical.'[153] According to the Task Group:

> Many clinicians have felt less and less able to influence decisions on the delivery of health care, while being held increasingly to account for the results of those decisions, or at least responsible for the outcomes. Many clinicians have decided to abrogate the responsibility for managing the health system at many levels, and just to get on with the clinical work. Many managers, left to make decisions without clinical expertise, feel less and less able to influence the clinicians who deliver the health care and who determine the quality and safety, and cost, of that care.[154]

In Ireland, the Commission on Patient Safety and Quality Assurance[155] and a number of HIQA reports have referred to issues within the health services relating to the lack of clinical leadership and the clinician–management divide. The Victorian Quality Council in Australia states that:

> Clinical leadership describes both a set of tasks required to lead improvements in the safety and quality of health care, and the attributes required to successfully carry this out. Visible and active clinical leaders can create a safety and quality programme that achieves positive and sustainable improvements for patients, and that fulfils the legal and ethical clinical governance obligations of health services.[156]

The HSE sets the discussion about clinical leadership firmly in the context of the imperative that exists in the light of failings identified within the system to achieve excellence in clinical governance. This takes an integrated approach to care and an integrated quality, safety and risk management framework. There are three components of the framework: first, the key system elements that service providers must have in place in order to drive safe and effective care; second, the core processes and programmes that lead to good outcomes; and, third, the performance indicators that demonstrate improvements in quality, safety and risk management, and link, where possible, to good outcomes for patients. This framework is represented in Figure 2; the components of the framework are modelled on Avedis Donabedian's 'structure, process, outcome' model.[157]

The HSE characterises clinical leadership as the glue that binds the elements of clinical governance together and believes that the implementation of the requirements contained in this framework will ensure that effective leadership and management is in place to drive forward the quality, safety and risk management agenda.[158]

The organisational changes that have been introduced into the HSE during 2008 and 2009 have led to the integration of health and personal social care across primary, community and acute care services. In addition, the new corporate structures have created a new directorate of quality and clinical care and the introduction of a new executive role of clinical director with delegated responsibilities and authority. In order to be able to guarantee effective clinical governance within these new structures and roles, there is a need, as demonstrated by Mountford and Webb in the *McKinsey Quarterly* article,[159] to develop a model of 'distributed' clinical leadership at corporate, regional, service, practice and front-line levels. The components of this model are represented in Table 2 (see page 118).

The HSE emphasises that the term 'clinician' is not confined to medical doctors. The delivery of optimal care and services to patients and service users efficiently relies, in many instances, on multidisciplinary teamworking, including social as well as health care professionals. Leadership will, therefore, be an important aspect of the work of all clinicians. Leadership will also be an important aspect of the work of non-clinical staff.

To complement the distributed leadership model described in Table 2, the HSE also provides a guide to the kind of qualities that are required for clinical leadership, in order to assist individual clinicians in developing their own leadership qualities. The list is

Figure 2: The HSE's Integrated Quality, Safety and Risk Management Framework

Outcomes

Outcomes

LEARNING AND SHARING INFORMATION
- learning from incident reviews
- learning from patient experience

SERVICE IMPROVEMENT
- identifying bottlenecks
- reducing inefficiencies
- reducing variation in key processes, e.g. discharge

Accountability

Assurance

Monitoring & Review

Patient/ Service User

Communication & Consultation

Capacity & Capability

Policies, Procedures, Protocols & Guidelines

PATIENT/ SERVICE USER AND PUBLIC/ COMMUNITY INVOLVEMENT
- patient information
- consumer panels
- patient experience surveys

STAFFING & STAFF MANAGEMENT
- workplace planning
- recruitment
- induction
- continuous professional development

RISK MANAGEMENT AND PATIENT SAFETY
- complaints/claims/incidents
- health and safety
- risk management process

CLINICAL EFFECTIVENESS AND AUDIT
- clinical guidelines

Outcomes

Outcomes

Source: HSE (2009b: 4), © HSE, 2009, reproduced with permission.

based on the NHS *Leadership Qualities Framework* website, which contains fifteen key 'generic' qualities based on feedback 'from hundreds of clinicians and managers in the NHS'.[160] The generic nature of the qualities contained in this framework is such that they can accommodate all clinical professions. They provide a framework of leadership that can unite clinical (and non-clinical) professionals in a shared leadership approach to clinical governance. Figure 3 illustrates the qualities referred to in the framework. The qualities are distributed across three clusters: personal qualities, setting direction and delivering the services.

The combination of the distributed clinical leadership model and the leadership qualities framework provides a clear and conceptually coherent platform applicable to all clinicians: medical, nursing

Table 2: The Essentials of Distributed Clinical Leadership

	Overall Identity	Sources of Power	Selected Leadership Skills and Knowledge Required
Corporate leader	• Clinician executive acting as steward of whole organisation • Little or no direct contact with patients	• Highly credible to colleagues as clinician and leader; able to communicate vision	• Corporate-level strategic thinking, talent management, succession planning • Political savvy, strong skills in negotiation and influence • Adherence to 'leadership qualities framework'
Regional and service leaders	• Passionate advocate for own region or service, takes responsibility for its clinical and financial performance • Moderate, little or no direct contact with patients	• Highly credible to colleagues, primarily as a clinician; well-connected, can tap into centres of excellence • Innovative, willing to take risks	• Fluent service management skills, e.g. strategy/people development and budgeting • Good knowledge of evidence-based medicine either generally or in own clinical area • Adherence to 'leadership qualities framework'
Frontline leader	• Great frontline clinician who focuses on delivering and improving excellent clinical care • High level of direct contact with patients	• Passionate about clinical work, credible to colleagues • Close to patients and frontline realities; can see opportunities for improvement	• Understanding of systems and quality improvement techniques, e.g. process mapping and operational improvement • Self-starter, able to work well in teams • Adherence to 'leadership qualities framework'

Source: HSE (2009b: 2), © HSE, 2009, reproduced with permission.

and other health and social care professionals. It also introduces a base set of leadership skills that will enable effective clinical governance. The HSE concludes by recommending that, in future, any clinical leadership development programme provided by the HSE should embed the model and leadership qualities framework outlined above.

Figure 3: NHS Leadership Qualities Framework

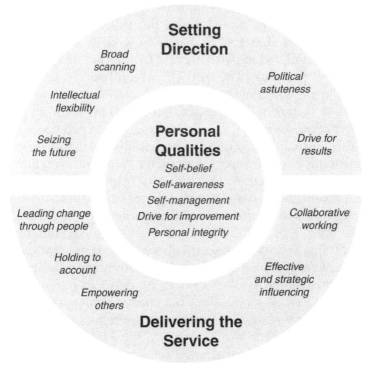

Source: NHS England (2006: 3), *The NHS Leadership Qualities Framework,* <http://www. nhsleadershipqualities.nhs.uk/portals/0/the_framework.pdf>, © NHS England, 2006, reproduced with permission.

HSE Quality and Clinical Care Directorate

Context

The full implementation of a robust quality, safety and risk management programme is one of the strategic objectives identified in the HSE's *Corporate Plan 2008–2011*. The plan proposed to establish a quality and clinical care directorate headed by a national director of quality and clinical care. This was intended to develop clinical leadership and clinical governance across the HSE and facilitate consolidation of the work carried out to date on the quality, safety and risk management agenda.

In January 2009, the HSE produced a working paper,[161] which set out the context, purpose, structure and functions of the new directorate. The working paper noted that the regulatory context in which health care is delivered in Ireland has changed radically in recent years. The HSRP of recent years had seen the establishment of the HIQA, which regulates health care providers – including the HSE – and the Mental Health Commission (MHC), which is also an external regulator of the care of mental health services. The working paper anticipated that the Irish health system would become increasingly regulated in patient safety by international authorities including the European Union (EU), which had already defined standards in areas such as blood safety.

Building a Culture of Patient Safety proposed the setting up of an implementation steering group, reporting directly to the Minister for Health and Children, with responsibility for progressing the recommendations of the report. Among these recommendations was the establishment of a licensing authority responsible for licensing services or institutions, based on compliance with national standards and with powers to approve and withdraw licences. The report also recommended the introduction of a system of credentialing individual clinical professionals, involving an objective evaluation of their current competence to practice, their training, experience and ability to provide particular services or perform particular procedures. These recommendations have far-reaching consequences for the HSE. They were among the reasons behind the creation of this directorate, which would prepare the HSE to operate in a regulated health and personal social service environment.

In addition, within the Department of Health and Children, the role of the chief medical officer (CMO) has been changed from an advisory role in policy areas to one that takes on executive responsibility for delivering specific reforms in patient safety and quality, and health promotion and public health.[162] The CMO is also the chairman of the implementation process for the patient safety commission report and is on record as saying that he wished to see all 134 recommendations 'set in train' within eighteen months.[163]

Purpose

The purpose of the directorate is to ensure that patients and clients of the health services in Ireland receive the best possible health and personal social care within available resources. According to the HSE working paper, the directorate is responsible for implementing the HSE's quality, safety and risk management framework.[164] There are three components in this framework.

The first component relates to the implementation of key structures, or 'underpinning requirements', such as communication and consultation processes; clear accountability arrangements; adequate capacity and capability to ensure quality, safety and risk management; standardised policies, procedures and guidelines; monitoring and review arrangements; and assurance processes.

The second component relates to the implementation of 'core processes and programmes' for clinical effectiveness and audits, including evidence-based practice; patient and public involvement; risk management and patient safety, including adverse event reporting; staffing and staff management; service improvement; and learning and sharing information.

The third component relates to developing and monitoring key performance indicators to demonstrate ongoing improvement in the quality, safety and risk management of care, and achieving the best possible health and personal and social services outcomes and to drive and demonstrate value for money. These assurances will be used internally as well as being provided to key external stake-holders such as the Department of Health and Children, the HIQA, the public and international bodies.

Functions

The working paper defined three key functions of the directorate. These are referred to as the SEA model: *Specify, Enable* and *Assure*. The directorate will be expected in the first instance to *specify* or determine standards for care quality, safety and risk management, together with related key performance indicators for the entire organisation, i.e. health and personal social services. It will also have an *enabling* function in building capacity to deliver on the quality, safety and risk management agenda by providing support, documented guidance, education, training and direct assistance to enable local service providers improve the safety and quality of care provided to patients/service users. Finally, the directorate will provide *assurance* to the CEO by monitoring compliance with key health and personal social services standards and performance against clinical and non-clinical indicators. These assurances must be capable of demonstrating to internal and external stakeholders that the best possible health and personal social care outcomes are being achieved for patients/service users within available resources. Ultimately, the directorate will be responsible for ensuring that the HSE has the capacity to operate effectively in the new context of increased external regulation (e.g. by the HIQA or the MHC) and the requirement for the licensing of providers of health and personal social services.

The implementation of all of the functions and activities of the quality and clinical care directorate will take a number of years. However, in June 2009 work on implementation was well underway, with the appointment of Dr Barry White as the HSE's first national director for quality clinical care.

The initial implementation of the work of the directorate was guided by a number of key operating principles. These included the importance of placing the patient at the centre of the work at all times; the need to pursue actions that can demonstrably improve organisational efficiency and effectiveness, evidenced by improved access and quality of services delivered to patients; the importance of combining central policy and strategy determination with the empowerment of local actors; simplicity and timeliness in all interventions aimed at improving services; and the importance of ensuring that everything that is done can be measured, is achievable, and is regularly monitored and evaluated.

With these basic operational principles in mind, it became apparent that there was a need to identify clear, measurable and time-framed objectives for the work of the directorate. It was agreed that the initial work should centre on issues of access, quality, economy and efficiency. This required the development of a methodology that focused on specific programmes, initiatives in clearly defined areas, to be developed in line with these parameters.

The emerging focus for these early initiatives included policy areas such as credentialing of individual clinical professionals as recommended by the commission on patient safety; targeted quality interventions (e.g. surgical check lists), intelligent support materials (e.g. documentation for framework, standards, guidelines, standard operating procedures and care pathways) capable of being used at the point of care by patients and clinicians; development of intelligent care pathways (defined as a pathway whereby the patient can access the right person and/or information at the right time and for the full spectrum of their journey); and intelligent resource planning by clinicians.

The directorate needed to identify areas of service delivery where they could have an immediate measurable impact. A number of areas of service focus for early initiatives and programmes were identified. These concentrated on specific diseases and treatments such as stroke (24/7 care, transient ischaemic attacks, use of anti-coagulants, stroke units, thrombolysis); cardiovascular disease (heart failure, arrhythmias, blood pressure/lipids, acute coronary syndrome); diabetes mellitus; COPD/asthma; epilepsy; depression (transfer of skills, reduced medication and hospital admissions); elective surgical activity (increased activity, reduction in length of hospital stay and elimination of waiting times); and acute medicine. These programmes were to be charged with delivering significant gains in access, quality and cost-effectiveness.

At the time of writing, the operational structure of the directorate was in development. Given the initial focus and the need for quick impact, it was becoming clear that there would be a need for an emphasis on value for money initiatives, quality and risk management initiatives and a focus on potential gains in the areas of drug utilisation. At the same time as the national director for quality and clinical care was appointed, a supporting appointment was made of a director for quality and risk management, reporting to the national director. Additional resourcing requirements for the directorate were being discussed at the time of writing.

Clinical Directorates and Mental Health

The policy context for the development of the mental health services in Ireland is contained in *A Vision for Change: Report of the Expert Group on Mental Health Policy.*[165] The implementation of the recommendations contained in the report is expected to happen over a period of seven to ten years. Each year the HSE sets a number of priorities related to the implementation process in line with the resources available. The implementation priorities for 2009 include the merging of existing mental health catchment areas to form expanded catchment areas with a population of approximately 300,000. These catchment areas are to be defined as integrated care service areas. Thirteen areas have been identified under the direction and management of regional clinical directors. It is believed that these larger catchment areas are essential to ensuring a more effective use of existing resources and delivery of the full spectrum of mental health services described in *A Vision for Change.*

This includes specialist services such as rehabilitation, mental health of intellectual disability (MHID) and forensics.

During 2009, the HSE indicated that it would establish clinical directors for each catchment area in accordance with the 2008 consultant contract, establish a single integrated management structure for all mental health services across the lifespan (i.e. child and adolescent, adult and older people), establish local multi-disciplinary mental health management teams where they do not already exist, and develop appropriate governance and account-ability arrangements for community mental health teams (CMHTs) in line with *A Vision for Change* and the 2008 consultant contract.

CHAPTER 8

Nursing and Midwifery and Clinical Directorates

A Question of Scale and Responsibility

One of the principal motivations for writing this book was to provide an opportunity to reflect on the implications for nursing and midwifery in Ireland of the introduction of the clinical directorate model in the Irish health services. This chapter sets out:

- To identify the issues that clinical directorates raise for nursing and midwifery and to take stock of relevant recent developments within the professions
- To identify the impact that the introduction of clinical directorates will have on the professions in the care settings in which they operate
- To list the principal implications for nursing and midwifery and make recommendations regarding the involvement of the professions in the development and implementation of clinical directorates and integrated services

The *Principles and Framework*[166] for clinical directorates produced by the HSE states that the success of the clinical directorates is dependent on the involvement of medical consultants in leadership positions as clinical directors with executive authority, working in a collaborative manner with other key staff including management, nursing and health and social care professionals. In addition, the guidelines on clinical leadership provided by the HSE[167] make it clear that while the clinical director provides clinical and executive leadership within the directorate all clinical professionals have a duty to provide leadership in their own specific areas of competence as part of multidisciplinary teams.

In order to appreciate the scale of what is being proposed by these multidisciplinary teams, organised in clinical directorates, it is useful to consider some statistics. Table 3[168] provides information on the number and percentage of personnel employed in the Irish health services by category for 2008.

Table 3: Health Service Personnel by Grade Category in Ireland (2008)

Grade Category	Number	Percentage
Medical/dental consultant	2,652	2.1
Medical/dental non-consultant	6,232	4.8
General support staff	15,334	11.9
Health and social care professionals	17,807	13.8
Management and administration	20,365	15.8
Other patient and client care	21,870	17.0
Nursing and midwifery	44,501	34.6
Total	*128,761*	*100.0*

Source: CSO (2009: 48, Table 6.12), data taken from HSE, *Service Personnel Census*, © HSE and CSO, 2009, reproduced with permission.

Medical consultants in Ireland represent just over 2 per cent of the health care workforce. The clinical directorate model, as it is implemented in Ireland, is predicated on the principle of clinical governance. In this model, the ultimate responsibility for clinical accountability rests on the shoulders of the medical consultants, acting as clinical directors. Other clinical professions must accept the duty of clinical accountability for their own area of expertise, but the ultimate onus of accountability rests with the clinical director. If this is going to work, it is essential that there is full cooperation from the other 98 per cent of the workforce.

Nursing and midwifery make up just over one-third of the health care workforce. If one excludes general support staff, management and administration, and considers only those who are directly involved in the provision of care to patients and clients, this rises to almost 48 per cent of the workforce (see Table 4).[169] However, when one considers the role of nursing and midwifery as being a coordinator of care and having responsibility for the inputs of those referred to as 'other patient and client care' personnel (including health care assistants, porters, emergency medical technicians, etc.), it is clear that the professions are responsible for over 70 per cent of the care providers within the health services. In addition, the involvement of nurses and midwives in care delivery requires them to be in direct contact with patients and clients twenty-four hours a day, seven days a week. This marks them out from all other professionals in terms of their impact on service delivery. They are also frequently directly responsible for the coordination and management of the inputs of the health and social care professionals in both acute and primary care settings.

Table 4: Health Service Personnel by Grade Category in Ireland (2008) (Excluding Management, Administration and General Support Staff)

Grade Category	Number	Percentage
Medical/dental consultant	2,652	2.8
Medical/dental non-consultant	6,232	6.7
Health and social care professionals	17,807	19.1
Other patient and client care	21,870	23.5
Nursing and midwifery	44,501	47.8
Total	*93,062*	*100.0*

Source: CSO (2009: 48, Table 6.12), data taken from HSE, *Service Personnel Census*, © HSE and CSO, 2009, reproduced with permission.

Nursing and midwifery are the lynchpins for the success of the clinical directorate model because of the pervasive nature of their role, the scale of their presence and the central position they occupy on behalf of the patient or client. The scale of the nursing and midwifery presence within the health services carries with it a heavy duty of responsibility to fulfil that professional role at all times in the best interests of the patients and clients of the service. Nurses and midwives are not just another group of employees among the more than 128,000 employees of the health services. They are the bulwark, the platform and the principal conduit through which care is provided to vulnerable and dependent patients and clients. Their professional code should make it imperative that they act at all times in the interests of patients and clients and never walk away from that duty of care no matter what. At a time of significant organisational change therefore, it is essential to understand the impact that that change will have on the professions in order to ensure that they are well positioned to fulfil the central role that is expected of them.

Framing the Issues

A New Culture

The *Principle and Frameworks*[170] document for clinical directorates states that, in determining the optimum clinical directorate model in any particular situation, the key considerations relate to population served, care pathways, existing or planned service configuration within the institution, network or region, and workload. A single directorate could cover more than one institution or entity, possibly even a national directorate for a particular specialty. Depending on local circumstances, it may be appropriate for some institutions to form part of a larger directorate model, rather than being stand-alone; however, proposed clinical directorates must give specific attention to linkages across the spectrum of primary, community and continuing care.

This represents a major cultural change in the provision of health services, away from an emphasis on the site to the service, defined in line with integrated care pathways and the patient journey. The determining factor in the configuration of directorates is not location but patient and care pathways, integrated on a national, regional or local basis. This has significant implications for nursing and midwifery. There will be a requirement for a greater degree of flexibility, working across primary and acute care settings and institutional boundaries, and organising workloads around the patient journey regardless of institutional settings. The new culture will manifest itself in the organisational structures that are being put in place for clinical directorates and the impact these will have on the management and delivery of services. The role of nurse managers within the clinical directorates and the role of the director of nursing will need to change to reflect this new culture. The work practices of front-line nurses and midwives at generalist, specialist and advanced practice will also need to reflect the new realities.

The emergence of a strong cohort of clinical leaders within nursing and midwifery in recent years as a result of the development of clinical career pathways introduces a new dynamic into the presence that the professions will have within this new cultural context. In the past, leadership for the professions has been expected from nurse managers at the level of director of nursing and midwifery, assistant director of nursing and midwifery and clinical nurse manager (or ward sister). There are now almost 100 advanced nurse/midwife practitioners and over 2,000 clinical nurse/midwife specialists within the services. Their presence offers new possibilities and for the professions to assert their clinical presence within the new configurations and organisational contexts. There will continue to be a need and requirement for strong leadership from within nursing management, but the clinical presence of nursing and midwifery offers new opportunities that must be grasped.

The Nursing and Midwifery Resource

The nursing and midwifery professions in Ireland are organised broadly across the five principal divisions of the register maintained by An Bord Altranais, i.e. registered general nurse (RGN), registered midwife (RM), registered children's nurse (RCN), registered mental health nurse (RMHN) and registered nurse intellectual disability (RNID). An Bord Altranais also maintains a register of nurses and midwives qualified to prescribe medications, known as registered nurse prescribers (RNPs). Nurses and midwives also have the opportunity to develop their clinical role at the levels of clinical nurse/midwife specialist (CNS/CMS) and advanced nurse/midwife practitioner (ANP/AMP). Nurses and midwives provide services at clinical and management level within institutions (hospitals, acute and long-stay care establishments, clinics, day centres, etc.) and within the community (primary care teams, GP practices, home-based services, public health services, mental health services, etc.). Nursing and midwifery presence in the community has traditionally been the domain of the public health nurse (PHN). As clinical roles within the professions have developed in recent years and as integration of services has gathered pace, this has changed.

In 2006 a report[171] by the School of Nursing, Dublin City University focused on identifying the core elements of nursing care deemed important for community registered general nurses. The report said that there were 430 nurses in the Irish Nurses Organisation (INO) database, whose primary role was to support the public health nurse (PHN) in community care in Ireland. The report stated that the Commission on Nursing had already raised concerns about the integration of the diverse range of nursing groups providing nursing services in the community and had stated that 'there is a need for the profession to develop a coherent vision for the future direction of nursing in the community which reflects the nursing needs of the community rather than the status of individual groups within the profession'.[172] This was the first substantial study on the role of the registered general nurse working in the community within Irish health care.

The professions also have a strong and growing academic base. Entry to the professions is at degree level and there are many post-graduate development opportunities up to Ph.D. and post-doctorate level. The work of the third-level educational institutions is complemented by the work of the centres for nurse and midwife education (CNE/CME) located within clinical settings, responsible for facilitating early pre-registration clinical education and post-registration continued professional development of the nursing and midwifery resources within their institutions. Opportunities for joint appointments between academic and clinical establishments are increasingly being encouraged within the professions and there are an increasing number of examples where this is happening. Research is also a growing area of nursing and midwifery activity and a concerted national strategy to increase and improve the quantity and quality of research in the professions is in place.

Many of the most significant developments in nursing and midwifery have taken place since the publication and implementation of the recommendations of the Commission on Nursing in 1998. Table 5 provides a summary of the key roles fulfilled by the professions within the health services in Ireland. The introduction of clinical directorates has implications for the professions across the whole spectrum of their presence within the health services.

Until 1998 there was no framework for developing a clinical career pathway for nurses and midwives in Ireland. It was the *Report of the Commission on Nursing* that recommended the establishment of a comprehensive clinical career pathway framework to encourage experienced nurses and midwives to remain in clinical practice and use their expert skills to improve patient outcomes and respond to health policy developments. The clinical career pathway leads from generalist to specialist to advanced practice. Levels on the pathway are linked with levels of educational preparation, responsibility and autonomy. The respective roles of staff nurses, staff midwives, CNSs, CMSs, ANPs and AMPs are distinguished by their scope of practice, educational preparation and levels of clinical decision-making, responsibility and autonomy. The National Council for the Professional Development of Nursing and Midwifery has defined the criteria and competencies for recognition at each stage along the career pathway in the form of a framework for the establishment of posts at clinical, specialist and advanced practice levels.[173] In June 2009, there were over 2,000 CNS/CMS posts within the health services and over 120 ANP/AMP posts.[174]

Table 5: Nursing and Midwifery Roles

Clinical (Hospital and Community)	Management (Hospital and Community)
Registered nurse (general, psychiatric, intellectual disability, children's)	Clinical nurse manager 1/clinical midwife manager 1 (CNM1/CMM1)
Registered midwife	Clinical nurse manager 2/clinical midwife manager 2 (CNM2/CMM2)
Palliative nurse	Clinical nurse manager 3/clinical midwife manager 3 (CNM3/CMM3)
Clinical nurse/midwife specialist	Nurse/midwife manager
Advanced nurse/midwife practitioner	Assistant director of nursing/midwifery
Public health nurse (community)	Director of nursing/midwifery
Practice nurse (community)	Assistant director of public health nursing (community)
(Research)	Director of public health nursing (community)

Education (Third-Level)	Education (CNE/CME)
College lecturer	Clinical placement coordinator
Statutory lecturer	Practice development coordinator
Senior lecturer	Tutor
Associate professor	Director of CNE/CME
Professor	(Research)
(Research)	

Joint Appointments
Clinical/academic/management joint appointments in nursing and midwifery

Source: Adapted from O'Shea (2008a: 23), © O'Shea, 2009, reproduced with permission.

The *Agenda for the Future Professional Development of Nursing and Midwifery*,[175] published by the National Council in 2003, highlighted areas for development within the nursing and midwifery professions for general, specialist and advanced practice. To date, many specialist roles in nursing and midwifery have developed around symptom management, diseases, treatments and health promotion. There are opportunities to identify other areas for specialist practice within nursing and midwifery that support holistic practice and enhance continuity of care. Specialist and advanced practice roles should be considered in all areas of nursing and midwifery practice where there is an identified health service need. The *Agenda* went on to identify how the role of the nurse and midwife could be developed in each of the branches of the professions, providing specialist nursing/midwifery services in a manner that reflects current health policy and responds to the needs of patients and clients. It stated that any developments should occur within an integrated service development framework and as part of an interdisciplinary approach to service delivery. The opportunity to do this within the framework of the clinical directorate model presents an opportunity to the professions to continue to develop their professional presence in line with the emerging service needs.

The National Council has published *An Evaluation of the Effectiveness of the Role of the Clinical Nurse/Midwife Specialist,*[176] which demonstrated that there was overwhelming support for the role of the CNS/CMS. The National Council also published *A Preliminary Evaluation of the Role of the Advanced Nurse Practitioner.*[177] Although limited because of the size of the sample involved, this evaluation provided preliminary evidence that ANP roles enhanced patient/client care by providing a holistic service that improved access to health care for patients/clients. They have also been widely accepted by patients/clients, nurses, doctors and other members of the multidisciplinary team. A more detailed evaluation of the role of the CNS/CMS and ANP/AMP was commenced in 2008 and is due to report in 2010.[178] This study will provide a comprehensive picture of the contribution that specialism and advanced practice is making to the effectiveness of nursing and midwifery in Ireland today. The evaluation report will identify clinical outcomes, service delivery (i.e. the service process) and economic implications in terms of the efficiency (outputs relative to cost) and effectiveness (outcomes relative to inputs) of services.

A Department of Health and Children report in 2001[179] recommended the introduction of the grade of health care assistant/maternity health care assistant as a member of the health care team to support the nursing and midwifery function. It was intended that the introduction of support workers should allow nurses and midwives to spend more time engaged in direct patient care. The report also recommended that appropriate provisions be made for the education and training of these support workers. As a result of the recommendations of the report,[180] a national pilot programme for the education of health care assistants was introduced in 2001. This consisted of a Level 2 training programme, developed specifically for health care assistants by FETAC (NCVA) (Further Education and Training Awards Council (National Council for

Vocational Awards)) in conjunction with key stakeholders. On conclusion of the course, participants were awarded a FETAC Level 2 health care support certificate. In 2002, an evaluation of the national pilot programme for the education of health care assistants was carried out[181] and the main recommendation was that, due to the success of the health care support certificate, it should be delivered again and should be developed and expanded to train all health care assistants across Ireland.

Additional initiatives in the training of support staff include the SKILL (securing knowledge intra lifelong learning) project,[182] which was set up in partnership between the trade unions and the HSE to provide education, training and development opportunities to staff working in support grades within the Irish health and personal social services. The project provides education, training and development initiatives to around 28,500 support staff and support service managers in the health services, including health care assistants, porters, catering assistants, household staff, semi-skilled persons/craftsperson's mates, maintenance persons, home supports workers, community carers, family support workers, general assistants, therapy assistants, speech and language assistants, laboratory aides and laundry staff.

Nursing and midwifery has come through a period of major development. It has a stronger, richer, more coherent professional presence within the health services. The development of clinical directorates presents opportunities for the professions to step up and take their place as leaders within this new organisational and cultural context. Leadership for the professions needs to come from both the management and the clinical side of the professions. Each one has a distinctive role to play within the new order.

Management in Nursing and Midwifery

There exists a clear structure for the management of nursing and midwifery in Ireland (see Table 5). At the apex of the profession is the director of nursing or midwifery, usually responsible for the nursing or midwifery resource within a hospital or institutional setting, and the director of public health nursing, responsible for the nursing and midwifery resource that operates within the community setting. There are about 40 posts for directors of public health nursing and about 268 posts classified as director of nursing.[183] The directors of nursing/midwifery were distributed across what are referred to as 'Bands', which reflect the relative size and complexity of the institutional setting. There are five Bands. Band 1 includes all of the larger acute and tertiary referral hospitals in the country. There are eleven hospitals included in this category. The remainder (Bands 2 to 5) range from large and medium-sized regional hospitals to small community-based units offering long-stay care of the elderly services. The use of the titles 'director of nursing' and 'director of midwifery' has been in place since the recommendation of the Commission on Nursing in 1998.[184]

Directors of nursing and midwifery have played a significant role in the development of nursing and midwifery services. They are supported proactively in this role by the National Council and by the nursing and midwifery planning and development units (NMPDUs), created on foot of a recommendation of the Commission on Nursing. The Commission reported that their consultations revealed the belief that senior nursing and midwifery managers concentrated on the individual management of nurses and midwives rather than the management of nursing and midwifery. It was suggested that they focused on such issues as the rostering of nurses and midwives, sick leave and annual leave rather than on the development of nursing and midwifery practice and policies for the more effective delivery of nursing and midwifery care. The Commission made a number of strong recommendations on the role of the director of nursing/midwifery, emphasising the importance of providing strategic clinical leadership and direction to the professions. In the years since the publication of the *Report of the Commission on Nursing*[185] the collaborative work that has evolved between the National Council, the NMPDUs and the directors of nursing and midwifery have resulted in many positive developments in the contribution that nursing and midwifery practices make to service delivery. The quantity and quality of nurse- and midwife-led services that have been developed (discussed later in this chapter), the development of over 2,000 clinical nurse and midwife specialists, the creation and approval of over 120 advanced practice posts in nursing and midwifery, and the embedding of a strong culture of degree-led education and continuous postgraduate professional development within the profession are all evidence of great progress in this regard.

Assistant directors of nursing/midwifery in both hospital and community settings usually take responsibility for the operational and professional management of divisions within institutions or community health care settings. They are usually supported in this task by clinical nurse/midwife managers (CNMs/CMMs), a central position in the operational management of front-line care. He or she is usually responsible for the management of a unit or ward within the institution. The CNM1/CMM1 is at assistant ward sister level and frequently deputises for the CNM2/CMM2. The CNM3/ CMM3 grade is used in institutional settings where there are a number of wards or units within a division, with a number of CNM2/CMM2 grade managers who require coordination. This might occur, for example, in a large acute care hospital where there are many operating theatres, each run by a CNM2/CMM2. The overall coordination of the nursing resource within the theatre services would then be the responsibility of the CNM3/CMM3.

The *Report of the Commission on Nursing* identified a number of perceptions that related directly to management and leadership within the professions. These were:

- A need for greater internal communication within organisations
- Nurses and midwives, and nursing and midwifery, were not sufficiently involved in strategic planning or in policy and strategy development
- A lack of partnership and consultation between general management and nursing and midwifery management and between nursing/midwifery management and nurses/midwives in setting and attaining corporate goals
- Nursing and midwifery managers were preoccupied with hierarchies and the detailed control of nurses and midwives rather than the management of the nursing and midwifery functions

The report identified a need to examine the recruitment, selection and training of nurse and midwife managers in order to ensure that the professions would have an effective cohort of leaders capable of responding to changing service needs. It also advocated greater devolution of authority within the nursing and midwifery management structures. These issues were also identified in a supplementary report prepared for the Commission on Nursing: *Management in the Health Services: The Role of the Nurse*.[186] Responding to this, the Commission made specific recommendations regarding internal communications within health service organisations, professional and personal career planning and the involvement of nurses and midwives in the strategic planning of the nursing and midwifery services. It also made recommendations regarding the roles of nurses and midwives in the management of their professions and their involvement in general management and emphasised leadership in both general management and clinical settings.

The Department of Health and Children subsequently establis-hed the institutional structures recommended by the Commission, and also set up a high level steering group on the empowerment of nurses and midwives. In September 2003, the Department issued the final report of the steering group, *Nurses' and Midwives' Understanding and Experiences of Empowerment in Ireland*.[187] The report made a number of recommendations regarding the develop-ment of practices and procedures that would lead to a more empowered workforce in nursing and midwifery. The recommen-dations were made under the headings of organisational development, management development, practice development and education. With regard to management development, the report referred to the work of the OHM[188] on nursing management competencies, which identified a number of key competencies required for each of the different levels of nursing management:

- At the top level:

  - Strategic and system thinking
  - Establishing policy, systems and structures
  - Leading on vision and values
  - Stepping up to the corporate agenda
  - Adopting a development approach to staff

- At middle management level:

  - A proactive approach to planning
  - Effective coordination of resources
  - An empowering and enabling leadership style
  - Setting and monitoring performance standards
  - Negotiation skills

- At front-line level:

  - Planning and organisation of activities and resources
  - Building and leading the team
  - Leading on clinical practice and service quality

- There were also generic competencies that should be present throughout nursing and midwifery:

- Promoting evidence-based decision-making
- Building and maintaining relationships
- Communication and influencing relationships
- Service initiation and innovation
- Resilience and composure
- Integrity and ethical stance
- Sustained personal commitment
- Practitioner competence
- Professional credibility

These competencies provide a description of what empowered, confident and professional nurse and midwife managers should look like and how they should behave. They are similar to the qualities identified in the distributed model of clinical leadership and the leadership qualities framework produced by the HSE, discussed in Chapter 7.

Clinical Directorate Structure

The clinical director profile that is included as part of the new consultant contract[189] states that each clinical directorate is headed by a clinical director, generally supported by a nurse manager and a business manager. This recognises the fact that the triumvirate model is the most effective structure for clinical directorates. It builds on the lessons learned and reported in Chapters 2 and 3 of this book and in particular the 1993 BAMM report, *Managing Clinical Services: A Consensus Statement of Principles for Effective Clinical Management*.[190] The triumvirate model also recognises the central role to be played by nursing and midwifery in ensuring that the clinical directorate is effective.

The consultant contract states that the primary role of a clinical director is to deploy and manage consultants and other resources, plan how services are delivered, contribute to the process of strategic planning, and influence and respond to organisational priorities. This includes responsibility for agreeing an annual directorate service plan, identifying service development priorities and aligning directorate service plans with hospital or network plans. In fulfilling this role, the clinical director will be supported by a business manager and nurse manager who will contribute to the planning and delivery of the services of the directorate and, in doing so, report directly to the clinical director.

According to the BAMM report, the most important factor in making clinical management effective is teamwork. The work of the clinical management team is multidisciplinary in nature and its effectiveness is dependent on recognition of the interdependence that this implies and the development of relationships, communications and confidence in each other's ability. The directorate management structure includes the clinical director, the nurse manager and the business manager. The wider team includes other consultant and non-consultant hospital doctors, the wider nursing and midwifery resource, the general support service staff and the health and social care professionals.

The BAMM report highlighted the role of the health and social care professionals (PAMs), which include social workers, physiotherapists, occupational therapists, dieticians, radiographers, pharmacists and others. It is important to ensure that they are integrated into the team structure and that their voice is heard in decision-making. In the past, as discussed in Chapters 2 and 3, some directorate configurations have resulted in this group forming their own clinical directorate with one of the professionals becoming clinical director. Alternatively, they are managed within a directorate with appropriate line management structures. Either model presents difficulties in ensuring integration into the team structure and raises the question of interaction between professional peers for support and the monitoring of professional standards. The same difficulties were faced by the early pioneers of clinical directorates in Ireland in St James's Hospital, Dublin, discussed in Chapter 3.

The role of the business manager was also described and discussed briefly in Chapter 3. Reporting directly to the clinical director, his or her responsibilities usually included managing clerical staff, managing the directorate office, business planning support, finance, identifying information needs and analysing information, and operational management of clerical and support staff. According to the BAMM report, business managers, like nurse managers, experienced a sense of isolation in their new roles. There is a need for support and development mechanisms to be put in place to assist them. The BAMM report highlighted the fact that most members of the management team within new clinical directorates feel ill-prepared for their new roles.

The nurse manager has responsibility for the professional and operational management of nursing services within the clinical directorate and is accountable for the nursing budget. He or she reports to the clinical director on all matters relating to the operation of the directorate. In effect this signals the end of the monodisciplinary silo model of nurse management in which all nurse managers report to a director of nursing. The model, therefore, has significant implications for nursing management. This represents a whole new way of working and reporting as part of a multi-disciplinary team. It will require the creation of a sub-unit culture at directorate level and an awareness that each member of the team is accountable to the clinical director for the budget and resources allocated.

The nurse manager in a large clinical directorate is likely to have a number of clinical nurse managers (CNMs) reporting to him or her. Depending on the complexity of the organisational structure and the care settings involved, these will include a mixture of CNM1s, CNM2s (formerly ward sister) and CNM3s, responsible for the front-line management of nursing services. The CNM is likely to have responsibility for a unit or ward, located within a specific institutional setting or in another location (e.g. small community-based units or day-care centres). The grades and roles need to be determined as part of the resource planning and service planning process. The nurse manager and the CNMs have responsibility for the management of the services within the directorate on a 24/7 basis. They are the key to the operational efficiency and effective-ness of the care delivery system. In addition, the nurse manager will have available CNSs/CMSs and ANPs/AMPs who provide high level clinical competence in nursing and midwifery within the care setting. Their role is different from and complementary to the role of the nurse manager and CNM. Their focus is clinical; they should never substitute for or take over the role of the nurse manager and CNM.

The development of the role of the nurse manager within the clinical directorate, where he or she is accountable for all matters related to the directorate to the clinical director, raises questions about the relationship he or she should have with the director of nursing. The traditional silo model of the professions was that nurse managers always answered to the director of nursing on all matters. The clinical directorate model changes this in a radical way. The relationship is one of professional accountability in areas such as quality, standards and safety of care. Chapters 2 and 3 of this book explore examples of how this has been developed in a number of settings. A closer examination of the role of the director of nursing and his or her relationship with nurse managers within a clinical directorate setting is provided later on in this chapter.

Over the last thirty years, many lessons have been learned about the introduction of clinical directorate structures. These lessons have been reviewed in Chapters 1, 2 and 3 of this book. The Brunel evaluation of the Resource Management Initiative[191] emphasised a number of important lessons:

- Involving clinicians in the management of resources was, first and foremost, about cultural change. The shift from the centre to the sub-unit of power and decision-making represents an enormous change for an organisation and those who work within it.
- In order to tackle the cultural change, it is essential to ensure that the change happens at the top of the organisation and that a strong sub-unit culture is encouraged, with service providers given budgetary responsibility. This sub-unit will need management and personal development support, including a comprehensive training and development strategy.
- Information is at the heart of the structure. The collation, analysis, dissemination and use of this information are greatly aided by the developments in information technology today.
- It is essential that key groups, nursing and health and social care professionals for example, are not marginalised or left to work in isolation. Their voice needs to be heard. It should be a strong voice, at the heart of the decision-making process.

In Ireland, the OPM's 2003 report for the OHM, *Learning from the NHS in Change*,[192] highlighted the key lessons to be learned from the UK experience in relation to the involvement of clinicians in management. These lessons include the importance of consultation and engagement as part of the change management process in order to address the significant human consequences of change; the importance of gaining buy-in by developing shared values, shared purpose and setting identifiable and realistic milestones and time frames; the need for a clear HR strategy and investment in the development of the key human resources; the importance of developing correct and appropriate infrastructure, including workforce capacity, organisational flexibility and ICT systems; and providing central leadership and direction balanced by local ownership and innovation. The report also echoed the Brunel emphasis on developing a new culture at the sub-unit level and moving away from the silo professional culture. A key part of this cultural change programme is the development and understanding of teamwork. The lessons learned from the survey of hospitals reported on in Chapter 3 provide additional endorsement of these key messages.

Clinical Leadership

The HSE's distributed clinical leadership model[193] (see Chapter 7) is applicable to all clinical professionals. The model is based on achieving excellence in clinical governance and this is something that can only be achieved if every member of the clinical team subscribes to the need for leadership within his or her own professional area of activity.

The distributed clinical leadership model describes the nature of leadership required at corporate level, regional and service level and front-line level.

The overall identity of a corporate leader is characterised as that of a clinician executive acting as steward of the whole organisation, with little or no direct contact with patients. The source of power of leaders at this level comes from their credibility with colleagues as a clinician and a leader capable of communicating a vision. The specific skills required at this level include corporate-level strategic thinking, talent management and succession planning. They also include political savvy and strong skills in negotiation and influence. The development of clinical corporate leaders in nursing and midwifery presents significant challenges to directors of nursing and midwifery and to the new leaders of clinical nursing and midwifery who have emerged in recent years (CNSs/CMSs and ANPs/AMPs). Both nursing and midwifery leaders will need to step up to the mark to provide leadership within and beyond the professions.

The overall identity of a regional service leader is characterised as being a passionate advocate for his or her own region or service and taking responsibility for its clinical and financial performance. At this level, the leader is likely to have moderate, little or no direct contact with patients. The source of power of a leader at this level also comes from credibility with his or her colleagues, primarily as a clinician, capable of tapping into centres of excellence. He or she should also be innovative and willing to take risks. The specific leadership skills and knowledge required include what the model refers to as fluent service management skills (e.g. strategy and people development, and budgeting). They also include a good knowledge of evidence-based medicine either generally or in his or her own clinical area. This is the level at which a nurse manager or senior nurse within a clinical directorate will have to operate.

The overall identity of a front-line leader is characterised as being a great front-line clinician who focuses on delivering and improving excellent clinical care. He or she will have a high level of direct contact with patients. The source of power of leaders at this level comes from their passion about their clinical work and the credibility this gives them with their colleagues. Leaders at this level are close to patients and front-line realities and can see opportunities for improvement. The specific leadership skills and knowledge required include an understanding of systems and quality improvement techniques (e.g. process mapping and operational improvement). They will also need to be self-starters and be able to work well in teams. Nurses and midwives at front-line level include generalist nurses and midwives, CNMs/CMMs, CNSs/CMSs and ANPs/AMPs. One of the stated objectives of the Commission on Nursing was to create a clinical career pathway that would be rich enough to encourage nurses and midwives to remain within the clinical setting while advancing their careers, rather than having to move to education or management to progress. This has been achieved and as a result there exists a rich resource of actual and potential front-line leaders within the professions today. Structures are now required however to facilitate their involvement at regional and national level on a shared basis that does not interfere with their contribution to the clinical setting, yet permits them to make a contribution to leadership at local, regional and national levels.

The distributed clinical leadership model is complemented by the leadership qualities framework (based on the NHS leadership qualities framework).[194] The qualities described in this framework are applicable at all levels of the distributed clinical leadership model and all leaders need to demonstrate adherence to them. The framework described qualities required at three levels. The first level refers to the personal qualities required of clinical leaders, including self-belief, self-awareness, self-management, a drive for improvement and personal integrity. The second level refers to the qualities required for setting direction. These include political astuteness, a drive for results, broad scanning, intellectual flexibility and seizing the future. The third level refers to qualities required for delivering the service. These include leading change through people, collaborative working, effective and strategic influencing, and holding to account and empowering others.

This framework provides a menu of opportunities for the development of nursing and midwifery leaders at all levels. It also provides a template for the assessment of candidates for leadership positions and a benchmark for the standards required of clinical leaders in nursing and midwifery. The qualities contained in the framework are not dissimilar to those that had already been identified in the *Report on Nursing Management Competencies* produced by the OHM in 2002.[195]

The HSE's quality and clinical care directorate (see Chapter 7) was set up with the intention of specifying standards, enabling the implementation of those standards and providing assurance that they are being implemented. As part of its enabling function the directorate has a role in building capacity to deliver on the quality, safety and risk management agenda by providing support, documented guidance, education, training and direct assistance to enable local service providers improve the safety and quality of care provided to patients/service users. Nursing and midwifery leaders and managers need to identify how they will work with the directorate to ensure that this enabling function is fulfilled in relation to the development requirements of the profession, particularly in the area of clinical leadership. Given the importance and scale of the nursing and midwifery resource within the health services, the staff of the quality and clinical care directorate will necessarily have to include senior nurses and midwives, capable of ensuring that the functions of the directorate are implemented within the professions and beyond. This should include nurses and midwives involved in the specifying, enabling and assuring functions of the directorate.

Nurses and midwives also have the potential to provide overall national and regional leadership through the functions of the quality and clinical care directorate by leading on the development and rollout of the work of the directorate. CNSs/CMSs, ANPs/AMPs and nurse and midwife leaders from within the management grades of the professions are ideal candidates to lead. This leadership would be on behalf of nursing and midwifery, as well as in partnership with representatives of all professions. By specifying the standards required, they would enable service deliverers and service managers to meet these standards. They would also monitor and audit their implementation as an essential ingredient in providing the assurance that is required to guarantee patient safety within the system.

Nurse-/Midwife-Led Services

As the role of nurses and midwives develops, there has been an increase in the requirement for, and the provision of, a wide range of nurse- and midwife-led services. Nurse-/midwife-led care is distinct from nurse-/midwife-coordinated or nurse-/midwife-managed services. An evaluation of the extent of nurse-/midwife-led services by the National Council, published in 2005,[196] stated that care is provided by nurses or midwives responsible for case management; the term 'case management' denoting comprehensive patient/client assessment, developing, implementing and managing a plan of care, clinical leadership and a decision to admit or discharge. Patients/clients are referred to nurse-/midwife-led services by nurses, midwives or other health care professionals, in accordance with collaboratively agreed protocols. This care requires enhanced skills and knowledge and the nurse or midwife needs preparation in both the clinical and management aspects of the role. Such nurses or midwives practise at an advanced level and may be working in specialist or advanced practitioner roles.

The issue of nurse-/midwife-led services is particularly relevant in the context of the development of clinical directorates, involving interdisciplinary teams and the relationships between acute, primary and specialised care settings. It is not a new concept in health care. In the UK, the NHS plan for investment and reform,[197] published in 2000, was explicit about the importance of nurse-led services based on the autonomy of the professions. The plan said that the old hierarchical ways of working were giving way to more flexible teamworking involving different clinical professionals. It identified a number of key roles for nurses and midwives:

- Ordering diagnostic investigations, such as pathology tests and X-rays
- Making and receiving referrals
- Admitting and discharging patients with specific conditions within agreed protocols
- Managing caseloads of patients with certain conditions (e.g. diabetes or rheumatology)
- Prescribing medicines and treatments
- Carrying out a wide range of resuscitation procedures including defibrillation
- Performing minor surgery and outpatient procedures.
  Triaging patients using the latest information technology

- Taking a lead in the way local health services are organised and managed

Many of these functions already exist in some services in Ireland and are envisaged as part of the more widespread changes that need to take place within the health services in Ireland in line with the HSE's transformation programme. The development of nurse-led services such as these can complement and enhance the development of clinical directorate structures that span primary and acute care settings.

The involvement of nurses and midwives in prescribing is a logical extension of all the other changes in the role that nurses and midwives are expected to play in the delivery of services. A national study by the National Council and An Bord Altranais was conducted on the involvement of nurses and midwives in the prescribing of medicines. The final report[198] of the study team recommended that prescriptive authority should be extended to nurses and midwives, subject to regulation. Legislation to enable nurses and midwives to prescribe has now been published. A nurse or midwife who completes the An Bord Altranais-approved prescribing education programme and meets the conditions emanating from the legal regulations may apply to An Bord Altranais to be registered in the new division as a registered nurse prescriber (RNP).[199] By June 2009, over eighty nurses and midwives had been registered as RNPs. The issue of prescription of medication raises the further question of the involvement of nurses and midwives in ordering radiology and laboratory services. Legislative provisions are in place to facilitate the implementation of nurse prescribing of ionising radiation (X-rays). The HSE is making arrangements for a phased implementation of these provisions. The introduction of this expanded practice for nurses with the authority to request ionising radiation is a significant initiative in the Irish health service and will have implications for the health care system as a whole, particularly in terms of access to services and expediting the patient journey.

The Impact of Clinical Directorates on Nursing and Midwifery

Delivering an Integrated Service
The introduction of clinical directorates is motivated by the desire to create a fully integrated health service that is adapted to the needs of the patient, guarantees patient and client safety and

delivers value for money in the use of resources. The configuration of clinical directorates is aimed at achieving that. The *Principles and Framework* document recognises that one solution does not fit all care or service need settings and encourages the development of models that are appropriate for and adapted to the specific local or regional needs. A strong rationale for a particular configuration is required for submission to the review forum responsible for the initial approval of clinical directorates and their subsequent review on an annual basis. However, all proposed configurations need to demonstrate that they are built on the principle of integration. Integration needs to happen, in the first instance within the institutions themselves. This will involve the bringing together of complementary areas of activity under one clinical director. It will also, where appropriate, mean integration between different institutions, involving the integration of smaller units located within the community, or local, regional and national units of service delivery within a particular specialty area. Boundaries of service delivery in institutional and community settings will, therefore, disappear. The emphasis is on the service, not the location of the service; the patient and the care pathway that he or she must travel and not on the administrative or institutional process.

A good example of an integrated service that has been developed in St James's Hospital, Dublin is the respiratory outreach programme[200] for the management of chronic obstructive pulmonary disease (COPD) in the community. Early discharge initiatives set up in 2002 for acute exacerbation of COPD evolved into comprehensive chronic respiratory disease programmes, managing all aspects of COPD in the community in a shared care model, while minimising in-patient care. The programme is based on the delivery of three levels of care (early discharge, day centre evaluation – optimisation of therapy, and pulmonary rehabilitation) by a single team, nurse- and physiotherapist-led, consultant- and GP-backed, seamlessly maintaining the patient in the community and taking the necessary hospital expertise into the patient's home in the process. A hospital-in-the-home care programme is delivered by a specialist respiratory nurse and a specialist respiratory physiotherapist, who install and manage home oxygen and nebulised bronchodilators, and manage ongoing steroid, antibiotic and other therapy until full recovery. The team, in close liaison with the GP, provides ongoing telephone support. The programme has resulted in a reduction in length of stay from an average 10.5 to 1.45 bed days. This results in a saving of 9 bed days per patient, 900 bed days per year, 3,600 bed days over 4 years, saving over €3 million. The patients have benefited from better disease control than traditional COPD outpatients department follow-up and a 75 per cent reduction in re-admission rates in one year.

The changes envisaged by this process of integration cannot happen without impacting significantly on the professions involved. The process of integration extends to the work practices and the divisions that have traditionally kept professionals in silos, answering to one of their own. Service integration requires professional integration, multidisciplinary cooperation and team-work. This will require a degree of flexibility and teamwork that is not to be found naturally in the health services as they have been traditionally configured. It represents an approach to service delivery that is based on flexible skill mix models, adapted to the needs of the patients. In the case of nursing and midwifery, it will include working with medical consultants, health and social care professionals and health care assistants as a matter of course and as part of a continuous team. It will also require of nurses and mid-wives that they work with the primary care teams and community intervention teams that have begun to emerge within primary care settings.

The challenge for nursing and midwifery is particularly considerable because of the scale of their presence within the system and the potential they have to coordinate and pull together the work of others for the benefit of patients. In order to promote a culture of integration across the professions, it will be necessary to consider the opportunities that exist for integrated education and training at both pre-registration and post-registration/continuous professional development levels. Educating, training and learning together on themes and topics of direct interest to the delivery of services can provide a platform for the formation of natural teams in the care setting and promote a culture of integration and cooperation.

The Director of Nursing/Midwifery

Integration of services within institutions and between institutions, within the community and between the community and institutions will result in the development of a corporate role for the director of nursing in the meaning contained in the distributed model of clinical leadership described earlier. The role of director of nursing/midwifery will span institutional and community boundaries. The director of nursing responsible for a group of clinical directorates in a region or speciality area of service will transcend institutional and community boundaries and will act as the clinical leader for all nurses and midwives under his or her span of control. This inevitably means that the role and functions of current directors of nursing/midwifery of smaller institutions (e.g. Bands 3, 4 and 5) will change in line with the service configuration within the clinical directorate structure. As these units become integrated into clinical directorate configurations for a particular area of service delivery, the nursing/midwifery management function will be configured in line with the clinical directorate structure and a senior nurse/midwife or clinical nurse/midwife manager will take responsibility as part of the nurse management team. Configuration of senior nursing/midwifery positions will change in line with the clinical directorate structure. This will most likely mean changes in competency requirements, titles and location. This is likely to take some time to evolve as the clinical directorate model is rolled out over the coming years.

It is also clear that the job descriptions and roles of the directors of nursing and midwifery will change. Responsibility for the operational management of the clinical nursing and midwifery resource will shift to the nurse/midwife manager within the directorate. The director of nursing/midwifery will be expected to provide a broader clinical leadership and strategic management role. The job descriptions of directors of nursing and midwifery within this new configuration of services are likely to expect him or her to:

- Be a member of the senior executive hospital management team (substitute community care setting as appropriate)
- In partnership with general management and clinical directors, develop, implement and monitor key performance indicators for nursing and for multidisciplinary teams
- Cooperate with clinical directors, nurse and midwife managers and senior hospital executives in determining an appropriate budget for nursing
- Develop innovative approaches to ensuring economy, efficiency and effectiveness in the use of resources in nursing and midwifery and other organisational areas in order to contribute to overall value for money within the service
- Develop local policy in alignment with national and strategic drivers in the management and development of staff

- Reconfigure services and associated resources according to changing patient and service needs
- Develop, lead and implement, in close cooperation with general management and clinical directors, the hospital's clinical governance strategy
- Be the principal professional adviser on all nursing and midwifery issues, including professional and clinical leadership, clinical governance, clinical supervision, professional practice and workforce planning
- Lead the development of nursing and midwifery roles at the levels of generalist, specialist and advanced practitioner in line with service needs; ensure that these roles are integrated fully into service development and implementation structures
- Lead in the development of the role of the nurse/midwife manager within the clinical directorate structure and provide ongoing professional support to nurse/midwife managers in the fulfilment of their role
- Ensure that modern standards of clinical nursing/midwifery care are in operation and that regular monitoring of nursing care is undertaken through audits
- Provide for appropriate formative, restorative and normative clinical supervision of nurses/midwives and nursing/ midwifery practice[201]
- Lead the nursing/midwifery profession, in cooperation with other health care professionals, in the development of integrated services spanning institutional and community boundaries, based on care pathways and the patient's journey
- Identify, develop and lead nursing/midwifery initiatives and new roles
- Provide leadership to all health care professionals in the areas of quality and patient safety
- Lead in the development of standards and practices in hygiene and infection control throughout all areas of service delivery
- Contribute to the regional and national development of health care policy and nursing and midwifery resources through participation in regional and national networks
- Ensure that the nursing/midwifery workforce is adequately resourced and educationally and clinically prepared to deliver high quality nursing/midwifery care in a changing and responsive organisation

- Develop relationships with third level educational institutions and, in partnership with other senior professional colleagues, develop multidisciplinary approaches to professional education and continuous professional development
- Lead in the development of research initiatives on behalf of nursing/midwifery and contribute to innovative approaches to multidisciplinary research
- Communicate effectively with a wide range of staff, including executive and divisional directors, clinical directors, lead clinicians, and senior clinical and non-clinical staff
- Build successful relationships across the acute and primary care settings, professional organisations, trade unions and staff at all levels
- Build and manage highly effective relationships with external partners, voluntary organisations, user and carer organisations, other health care delivery structures and educational institutes

Of course, job descriptions will vary from one clinical care setting to another and from one discipline or area of speciality to another. The overarching trend however is towards a situation where the director of nursing/midwifery is responsible for the management of nursing/midwifery, not nurses/midwives. His or her contribution to clinical leadership and clinical governance issues and supporting the nurse/midwife managers responsible for the operational management of the nursing/midwifery resource is a key part of the role. He or she will also be responsible for ensuring that there is a well-articulated nursing voice at the corporate decision-making table, capable of negotiating budgets for the nursing and midwifery resource for the corporate structure. He or she will lead in the integration of services and the development of cooperative, multidisciplinary approaches to service development with the interests and safety of the patient at the core.

In the mental health services, as reported in Chapter 7, the creation of thirteen integrated care services areas within the newly defined mental health catchment areas and the appointment of a clinical director for each catchment area in line with the 2008 consultant contract have significant implications for senior nursing management in mental health. The configuration of these clinical directorates and the definition of roles for the nurse managers within them will evolve over time and are likely to impact on the role, functions and location of directors of nursing in the mental health services.

The development of a senior nursing/midwifery role such as this within corporate structures of service delivery in both mental health and other health care areas seems to call out for the creation of a senior nursing/midwifery resource, with appropriate skills and competencies, within the HSE's quality and clinical care directorate at both national and regional level. This will ensure that nursing and midwifery play a full role in the specifying, enabling and assuring functions of this directorate.

The Nurse/Midwife Manager

The nurse manager is a key member of the triumvirate clinical directorate management team as described in the clinical director profile included in the consultant contract.[202] He or she is operationally accountable to the clinical director on all matters that refer to the management of the nursing/midwifery resource within the clinical directorate. He or she has a professional relationship with the director of nursing/midwifery in all matters of professional standards, quality and development of nursing services. His or her role, together with that of the business manager, is to support and cooperate with the clinical director in the overall planning and management of the directorate. His or her job description is likely to require him or her to:

- Report directly to the clinical director on all operational matters under his or her control pertaining to the work of the directorate
- Contribute to the process of strategic planning for the directorate in nursing/midwifery and nursing-/midwifery-related matters
- Contribute to the preparation and negotiation of the directorate service plan, identifying service development priorities and aligning them with hospital or network priorities
- Reconfigure services and associated resources according to changing patient/service needs
- Lead the development of nursing and midwifery roles at the levels of generalist, specialist and advanced practitioner in line with service needs. Ensure that these roles are integrated fully into service development and implementation structures within the directorate
- Assume accountability and responsibility for the nursing/midwifery budget and for the management of the nursing/midwifery resource within the directorate

- Develop innovative approaches to ensuring economy, efficiency and effectiveness in the use of resources in nursing/ midwifery and other areas in order to contribute to overall value for money within the directorate
- Provide professional and clinical leadership to the nursing resource within the directorate in accordance with service needs
- Monitor and control actual performance against planned targets for the resources under his or her control
- Lead the implementation of quality assurance, risk management and patient safety control mechanisms in line with agreed national and regional protocols, including cooperation with all clinical audits as required
- Work as part of a team and promote a culture of teamworking within the directorate across all professions
- Cooperate closely with other clinical professionals in achieving the objectives of the directorate
- Contribute to effective communication within the directorate, across the hospital or service and with external stakeholders
- Support clinical training and continuing professional development for the nursing/midwifery resource within the directorate and cooperate with other senior professional colleagues in the development and implementation of multidisciplinary professional development and training initiatives
- Lead the development of research initiatives on behalf of nursing and midwifery within the directorate and contribute to innovative approaches to multidisciplinary research

In acute care settings, nurses/midwives and managers should have an input into areas of service management and delivery that affects the delivery of nursing and midwifery services. This should include involvement in bed management, where the role of nurses and midwives and their broad knowledge and understanding of the services equip them to play a distinctive role. It should also include involvement in quality development initiatives where nurses and midwives have frequently taken a lead role. In addition, it should include, where appropriate, inputs into the control and management of services of hygiene, laundry, catering and other logistical activities that affect the total quality of care for the patient/client in the acute care setting. The involvement of nurses and midwives in these areas should be agreed in accordance with management protocols developed at the local level in accordance with service and professional development needs.

The precise description of the role of the nurse/midwife manager is likely to vary from one care setting and one speciality to another. The overarching theme however is one of integrated, multidisciplinary teamwork, reporting to the clinical director and maintaining a professional link on behalf of the nursing/midwifery resource with the director of nursing/midwifery. The nurse/midwife manager is also a senior executive within the directorate with budget and accountability responsibility delegated from the clinical director. He or she needs to be empowered to take control over the environment for which he or she is responsible and to take decisions about the management of that environment in the interests of quality of care, patient safety and best use of resources available.

The Clinical Nurse Midwife Manager

The role of the CNM2/CMM2 will continue to be of central importance within the clinical directorate structure. He or she will be responsible for the management of a unit or ward and will, in the majority of cases, provide the key front-line management needs of nurses and midwives in the care setting. The Commission on Nursing defined the functions of clinical nurse managers/clinical midwife managers as:

- Providing professional and clinical leadership
- Staffing and staff development
- Resource management
- Facilitating communication

The CNM2/CMM2 should be empowered by the nurse/midwife manager to fulfil all the key front-line management functions within a unit or ward. In order to do that, he or she will require the provision of appropriate information and training and should be involved in determining the resource needs for the unit. The CNM2/CMM2 is usually supported where necessary by a CNM1/CMM1, who will deputise for the CNM2/CMM2 when necessary and provide additional management support in complex care delivery settings. In occasional circumstances (e.g. in large accident and emergency department or large surgical/operating units within large acute hospitals), there may also be the need for a CNM3/CMM3 to provide departmental management cover. The determination of the precise combination of grades required for a particular care setting is a matter for service planning at a local level with the clinical directorate.

The Nurse/Midwife

The backbone of care delivery within the health services will continue to be provided by the tens of thousands of nurses and midwives who operate at the front line in acute and primary care settings. The level of practice at which individual nurses or midwives act will depend on where they are in the clinical career pathway, i.e. at generalist, specialist or advanced practice.

A CNS/CMS works in a defined area of nursing or midwifery practice that requires the application of specially focused knowledge and skills, which are in demand and are required to improve the quality of patient/client care. This specialist practice encompasses a major clinical focus, which comprises assessment, planning, delivery and evaluation of care given to patients/clients and their families in hospital, community and outpatient settings. CNSs/CMSs work closely with medical and paramedical colleagues and may make alterations in prescribed clinical options along agreed protocol-driven guidelines. They also participate in and disseminate nursing/midwifery research and audits and provide consultancy in education and clinical practice to nursing/ midwifery colleagues and the wider interdisciplinary team. The core elements of specialist nursing and midwifery practice are clinical focus, patient/client advocacy, education and training, audits and research, and consultancy.[203] ANP/AMP roles are developed in response to patient/client needs and health care service requirements at local, national and international levels and are carried out by autonomous, experienced practitioners who are competent, accountable and responsible for their own practice. They are highly experienced in clinical practice and promote wellness, offer health care interventions and advocate healthy lifestyle choices for patients/clients, their families and carers in a wide variety of settings, in collaboration with other health care professionals, according to the agreed scope of practice guidelines. They utilise advanced clinical nursing/midwifery knowledge and critical thinking skills independently to provide optimum patient/client care through caseload management of acute and/or chronic illness. The core elements of advanced nursing and midwifery practice in Ireland are autonomy in clinical practice, expert practice, professional and clinical leadership, and research.[204] As clinical directorates expand and become the norm, nursing and midwifery will operate on the basis of a primary–acute care continuum, moving seamlessly between acute and primary care settings in line with the needs of the patients and the patient journey. The modalities of this will need to be agreed with local health service managers or clinical directors and there will be a need to define appropriate protocols. These will include developing the role of nurses and midwives as active members of primary care teams in cooperation with GPs and other community-based health care professionals.

As part of their role within the primary–acute care continuum, nurses and midwives will continue to develop nurse-/midwife-led clinical services. These services should be developed in consultation with the clinical director and other health service managers, and should reflect the levels of practice of the individual nurse or midwife. They should include as appropriate:

- Management of case loads in both acute and community settings in accordance with agreed practice protocols and in line with their levels of practice
- Management of early discharge from acute settings and follow up with the patient/client in the community including, where appropriate, in their own home
- Diagnosis of conditions in accordance with agreed practice protocols
- Treating and prescribing in accordance with agreed practice protocols
- Referring clients/patients to other areas of service delivery and other professionals in accordance with the needs of the patient/client
- Taking referrals from other areas of the services and from other professionals in accordance with the needs of the patient/client
- Education and empowerment of patients/clients in community settings and in their own homes in the management of their own health

Nurses and midwives will prescribe medications in accordance with the provisions of legislation and after having completed the required education and training programmes and having achieved registration as an RNP with An Bord Altranais.

Nurses and midwives will incorporate the roles of health care assistants, home helps and other support staff into the delivery of their services as appropriate in both acute and primary care services, and in line with agreed protocols and practice. They should also continue to develop relationships with medical consultants, doctors and other health care professionals in a way that reflects the development of their roles within their career pathways and in line with service needs. This should include identification of complementarity, development of an understanding of what each professional can bring to a multidisciplinary team, breaking down silos of practice and encouraging a culture of common decision-making, collaborative working and multidisciplinary service delivery.

Implications and Recommendations

While this book has sought to engage all professionals involved in the clinical directorate concept, one of the main motivations for writing it came from the desire of the author to reflect on the implications for nursing and midwifery in the Irish health services. Some of the key implications for nursing and midwifery can be summarised as follows:

1. **Patient focus**: The vision for integrated health and social care services for the future in Ireland is one that is centred on the patient. This patient focus will concentrate on the centrality of the patient journey. It will also emphasise the importance of quality and risk management in the development and delivery of services within the framework of efficient and effective management of resources. Clinicians (including nurses and midwives) will be responsible and accountable for delivering quality, safe care to patients within the limits of the resources that are available. Nursing and midwifery occupy a central role in the provision of health services in Ireland. This will become even more apparent as the clinical directorate structure is implemented across all health care settings. The nursing and midwifery professions must accept the responsibility and duty that go along with this central position and continue to develop a professional culture that is accountable and driven by the fundamental demands of patient safety. This is a requirement of their professional role within the health services and the duty of care they have to patients and clients of the services. The professions of nursing and midwifery are patient-centred, relationship-based, holistic approaches to care, involving the provision of education and information to patients and their families, coordination and advocacy on their behalf and continuity of care. The

professions are based on acquired knowledge, skills and clinical judgement accumulated through study, research, observation and reflection. They are dedicated to ensuring the quality and safety of care for patients, improving access and building the capacity to deliver care where it is most needed. This is the contribution that nursing and midwifery can make to the Irish health services through the clinical directorate structures.

2. **Multidisciplinary teams**: The clinical directorate model represents the breaking down of professional silos. The management and delivery of clinical services will be done through integrated multidisciplinary teams. This represents a change in the nature of reporting relationships for nurses and midwives within the services. The overall leadership and accountability within the clinical directorate structure is with the clinical director as described in the consultant contract. Clinical professionals will, however, be responsible for providing clinical leadership as part of the team from the perspective of their own discipline. Nurses and midwives will occupy central roles in these teams, through the role of the nurse manager within the directorate and nurses and midwives at all levels of practice. The clinical directorate model breaks down barriers between professions. Nurse and midwife managers will now be reporting to the clinical director and will be expected to work as members of a team with the business manager and other key professionals within the directorate structure. This will require the development of a new culture and new skills for nurse and midwife managers. It also requires acceptance of the fact that medical consultants occupy a central role in the clinical directorate model as ultimate accountable persons for the activities of the directorate. This requires the creation of a culture of professional collegiality in the management of this onus of accountability.

3. **Director of nursing**: The role of the director of nursing will no longer be institution based. He or she will span institutional boundaries, operating across institutions and into the community. The director of nursing is likely to have responsibility for a number of clinical directorates within a region. The role will be strategic and will focus on the professional, clinical leadership, quality and risk manage-

ment issues that face the professions. He or she will work closely with other senior clinical professionals to support the rollout of integrated services and the role of nursing and midwifery within them. The inclusion of nurse/midwife managers as part of the structure of clinical directorates means that the onus for the management of the nursing and midwifery resource at the front line shifts to the local nurse manager. This will require senior nurse/midwife management to fill a wider strategic role on behalf of the profession at regional and corporate level. The competencies, functions, titles and numbers of senior nurse and midwife managers are all likely to change as the clinical directorates develop. The national leaders of nursing and midwifery will need to step forward and occupy these key posts and represent the professions as their voice in a credible manner.

4. **Nurse managers**: Within the clinical directorate structure, nurses and midwives will have complete control over the environment within which they operate and deliver care. They will be accountable for budgets and resource management at a local level and will be empowered to allocate resources in the best interests of patients. They will also be required to operate within agreed budget and resource management limits as set out in the clinical directorate service plan and agreed with the clinical director. This implies the development of appropriate skill sets to ensure that nurse managers are capable of fulfilling this role. The role of the nurse manager within a clinical directorate will span institutional and community boundaries and is likely to involve managing nursing and midwifery resources in more than one location. Nurse managers within the clinical directorate and the team of clinical nurse managers they have around them will be empowered by the clinical directorate structure to configure and develop the deployment of the nursing and midwifery resource in line with the priorities defined in the clinical directorate service plan. The nurse/ midwife manager will be expected to provide clinical and operational leadership to the profession within the directorate. This has the potential to significantly enhance the impact that local nursing and midwifery management can have on the quality of care that is provided.

5. **Nurses and midwives**: Generalists, specialists and advanced practitioner nurses and midwives will work in a flexible manner across institutional and community boundaries. They will lead and develop services in partnership with other clinical professionals, within the institutions and the community, for the benefit of patients and clients. They will work in line with agreed quality and safety frameworks and protocols agreed at national, regional and local levels. They will bring into the community the benefits of the systems and structures that exist within the acute services and they will follow the patient journey in accordance with agreed protocols and resource management criteria. Expansion of the roles of nurses and midwives at all levels of practice will be encouraged and supported. The clinical directorate model empowers front-line generalist, specialist and advanced practitioner nurses and midwives to lead in the design and implementation of care adapted to the needs of patients and clients, in a manner that reflects their care pathways and integrates the delivery of that care across institutional boundaries. The pre-registration, post-registration and professional development opportunities available to nurses and midwives in today's Irish health services mean they have a unique opportunity to position nursing and midwifery as confident professions capable of taking their place alongside all other clinical professions as members of the multi-disciplinary team.

6. **Quality and clinical care directorate**: Nurses and midwives should be involved in the national quality and clinical care directorate to work with other clinical professionals in the rollout of the work of the directorate. This will involve them in mapping out patient journeys in care- and disease-specific areas and producing guidelines, frameworks and standards for the delivery and management of care at regional and local levels. They will be responsible for rolling out development and implementation programmes in cooperation with staff in the offices of the regional operations director and in individual clinical directorate settings. This work will include defining rules, care pathways, resource management guidelines, efficiencies and incentives to guide clinicians in the delivery of their services. They will also be responsible for

the development of intelligence and information systems, based on standardised cross-disciplinary coding of activities within case-mix settings. This will involve the preparation of information materials supported by manuals and guides. They will also facilitate the HIQA in the definition and interpretation of standards and the implementation of licensing and credentialing procedures and processes. The nurses and midwives within the quality and clinical care directorate will include a core team of full-time staff assisted by teams created for specific projects. This should facilitate the use of secondments and joint appointments for specific periods of time for nurses and midwives from clinical settings at generalist, specialist and advanced practice levels and at clinical nurse manager level where appropriate. Appropriate structures at national, regional and local level will need to be developed to enable this to happen.

7. **Regional operations**: The regional operations director will need to involve nurses and midwives at appropriate levels to assist in the reconfiguration of services in line with the new model of service delivery, the delivery of integrated services in line with the nationally defined frameworks, standards and resources, and the resourcing and supporting of clinical leadership in service delivery. This will involve secondment arrangements for nurses and midwives from clinical settings at generalist, specialist and advanced practice levels and at clinical nurse management levels assigned to specific care and disease settings on a project basis.

CONCLUSION

A Challenge for all Professions

This book has looked back at the history of clinical directorates as they developed in the US, the UK and in Ireland over the past thirty years. It has reached the critical point in that journey in Ireland where, in 2008, the clinical directorate model was placed at the heart of the new consultant contract and became the accepted model for the configuration of health services in Ireland for the foreseeable future.

The rollout of the clinical directorate model based on these core concepts is a major undertaking that will take a number of years to implement. The historical review contained in this book and the review of the reports, guidelines and discussion papers that have informed recent developments in Ireland all contain lessons about what needs to be borne in mind as we embark on this path. At the conclusion of this book, it is perhaps worthwhile to take some time to gather together some of those key lessons and to list them as a reminder of what needs to be done if we are to be successful in the transformation of the health services that is intended. The key lessons include the following:

1. **The cultural challenge**: The introduction of clinical directorates is first and foremost a cultural challenge. It involves the devolution of power and responsibility from the centre to sub-units and the consequent empowerment of professionals to make decisions. This shifts the emphasis away from the top and the centre towards the sub-units and requires the development of a strong culture of identity within the clinical directorate sub-unit. The culture of the sub-unit needs to be one of professional accountability, teamwork, integration and empowerment as these values translate themselves throughout the whole system.

2. **Inclusiveness**: The success of the clinical directorate model is built on the imperative of involving all professionals, avoiding the marginalisation of key groups such as nursing

and health and social care professionals. In the Irish system, where the emphasis is on the pre-eminence of the medical consultant acting as clinical director and the contractual implications of this role, there is a danger that other professionals are not engaged with in the design, development and implementation of appropriate configurations at a local level. This will result in marginalisation that will militate against the ability of the structures that are created to deliver the kind of integrated care that is envisaged by the clinical directorate model. For these reasons, it is important to engage all clinicians around the central concepts and challenges of professional accountability and whole systems approaches such as clinical pathways and the patient journey. Every profession has a role to play in these pathways and along the steps of the patient journey. Their individual role and contribution must be respected and integrated from the start.

3. **Structure**: There is no one-size fits-all model. Different care settings, specialties, geographic locations and cultural environments will require modifications in the configuration of the basic clinical directorate model in order to adapt to local idiosyncrasies. The development of the most appropriate configuration requires consultation and inclusiveness across all professional boundaries.

4. **Communication**: Good communication is essential at all stages of the design and implementation of clinical directorates. This includes consultation with and inclusiveness for all professionals. It also includes the design and implementation of comprehensive information management systems suitable for their purpose in an age of sophisticated ICT potential. It includes the use of information technology to break down barriers between institutional and community care settings and to introduce economies and efficiencies into the management and delivery of services across professional and institutional boundaries. Information flows are also a key component of patient safety and form the material on which good clinical audits are based in the interests of patient safety.

5. **Training and development**: Clinical professionals are not necessarily good managers. Evidence throughout the years presented in this book suggests that most clinical managers feel ill-prepared for the role they have undertaken in the clinical directorate structure. The provision of initial and

ongoing training and development support, designed to meet the needs of local managers, is an essential pre-requisite to success. It helps to combat the sense of isolation that most clinical managers feel, particularly at the beginning of the implementation process.

6. **Governance**: Accountability is at the heart of the clinical directorate model. This includes clinical and professional accountability for practice. It also includes accountability for the use of resources. All of this requires the development and implementation of systems capable of providing the necessary assurances at all levels within the system.

7. **Management of change**: Implementing clinical directorates requires sophisticated project planning, including provisions where necessary for the maintenance of parallel systems during an introductory period of system change. It also requires careful management of the human impacts of the change process using best practice change management techniques. The creation of change management teams at regional and local levels can assist in ensuring an effective rollout with the maximum level of engagement and participation from all key players.

On a concluding note, the introduction of clinical directorates in the Irish health services is in its early stages. Progress to date, as this book has shown, has been significant and was eloquently summed up by the Minister for Health and Children, Mary Harney, TD, speaking at the University of Limerick in January 2009:

> The greatest asset of our system is the knowledge and capacity of the people who work within it. We need to encourage, support and indeed require clinicians – doctors, nurses and other professionals – managers and other health care workers to deliver the best possible services to their patients. We want to empower local decision-making within a coherent national policy framework and governance structures. I have been a strong supporter of the involvement of clinicians in leading change, in being part of management, in the organisation of services and the best use of resources. Clinical involvement in management, reform and innovation is one of the most powerful forces for improvement. I have seen brilliant and dedicated clinical leadership throughout the health services – often not recognised. There's an old cliché about not cursing the darkness but lighting a candle – truly, though, the satisfaction and the progress made when candles are lit by clinicians with management and staff together is worth all the effort.[205]

ENDNOTES

Introduction
[1] O'Shea (2008a).
[2] Madden (2008).

Chapter 1 – The Resource Management Initiative in the UK
[3] Beveridge (1942).
[4] Rivett (2009).
[5] Donaldson and Muir Gray (1998).
[6] Dyson (1984: 255).
[7] Griffiths (1983).
[8] DHSS (1986).
[9] Spurgeon (2001).
[10] DHSS (1986).
[11] Buxton et al. (1989).
[12] Department of Health (UK) (1989).
[13] Buxton et al. (1991).
[14] Packwood et al. (1991).

Chapter 2 – The Emergence of Clinical Directorates
[15] OHM (2001a).
[16] OHM (2001a).
[17] OHM (2001a).
[18] OHM (2001a).
[19] Hopkins (1993).
[20] Packwood et al. (1991).
[21] Kennedy (2001).
[22] Chantler (1994: 3).
[23] BAMM et al. (1993).
[24] Fitzgerald (1991).
[25] Her Majesty's Government (1990).
[26] Department of Health (UK) (1998).
[27] Department of Health (UK) (2000).
[28] Garelick and Fagin (2005).
[29] Disken et al. (1990).
[30] For example, Rea (1995) and White (1993).
[31] Disken et al. (1990).

32 Maxwell (1993).
33 Rea (1995).
34 Rea (1995).
35 Disken et al. (1990).
36 BAMM et al. (1993).
37 Edmondstone and Chisnell (1992).
38 Disken et al. (1990).
39 Disken et al. (1990).
40 Royal College of Nursing (1990).
41 Maxwell (1992).
42 Gupta et al. (2008).
43 Gupta (2005).
44 Goodwin (1996).
45 Thorne (1997).
46 Gupta et al. (2008).
47 Harvey (2007).
48 Department of Health (1947).
49 Department of Social Welfare (1949).
50 Department of Health and Children (2003a).
51 OPM (2003).
52 Iles and Sutherland (2001).

Chapter 3 – Early Examples of the Implementation of Clinical Directorates

53 O'Shea (1995).
54 Government of Ireland (1961).
55 Department of Health (1971); Department of Health (1984).
56 Fitzgerald (1968).
57 O'Shea (1995).
58 O'Shea (1995).
59 O'Shea (1995).
60 O'Shea (1995).
61 O'Shea (1995).
62 O'Shea (1995).
63 O'Shea (1995).
64 BAMM et al. (1993).
65 O'Shea (1995); St James's Hospital (1992).
66 O'Shea (1995).
67 O'Shea (1995).
68 O'Shea (1995).
69 Her Majesty's Government (1990).

70 Department of Health (UK) (1989).

Chapter 4 – Health Service Reform in Ireland
71 Government of Ireland (1970).
72 Harvey (2007); Barrington (2000).
73 Department of Health (1994).
74 Department of Health (1994: 10).
75 Department of Health (1986).
76 WHO (1981).
77 Commission on Health Funding (1989).
78 Kennedy (1991).
79 Hickey (1990).
80 Department of Health and Children (2001a).
81 National Task Force on Medical Staffing (2003).
82 Commission on Financial Management and Control Systems in the Health Service (2003).
83 Department of Health and Children (2001b).
84 Department of Health and Children (2002).
85 Department of Health and Children (2004).
86 Prospectus Strategy Consultants (2003).
87 National Task Force on Medical Staffing (2003: 126).
88 National Task Force on Medical Staffing (2003: 103).
89 Department of Health and Children (2003a).
90 HSE (2008a).
91 Government of Ireland (2004).
92 Government of Ireland (2004).
93 HSE (2008a).
94 Public Services Organisation Review Group (1969).
95 HSE (2006).
96 HSE (2006: 5).
97 HSE (2008b).
98 Department of Health and Children (2009a).
99 Department of Health and Children (2009a).
100 Department of Health and Children (2009a).
101 HSE (2008c).
102 HSE (2008d).
103 Drumm (2008).
104 Donnellan (2009).
105 Department of Health and Children (2009a).
106 Department of Health and Children (2008:11).

Chapter 5 – Patient Safety and Patient-Centred Care

[107] Madden (2008).
[108] Harding Clarke (2006).
[109] Madden (2008: 39).
[110] Madden (2008: 39).
[111] Madden (2008: 3).
[112] Madden (2008: 11).
[113] Department of Health and Children (2008).
[114] HIQA (2008a: 4).
[115] HIQA (2008a).
[116] National Council (2006).
[117] Field and Lohr (1990).
[118] Field and Lohr (1990); Keeley (2003).
[119] NICE (2007).
[120] New Zealand Guidelines Group (2001).
[121] Hewitt-Taylor (2003); Mc Sherry and Taylor (2003).
[122] Hewitt-Taylor (2003).
[123] Madden (2008: 69).

Chapter 6 – The Establishment of Clinical Directorates in Ireland

[124] OHM (2001a).
[125] OHM (2004a).
[126] OHM (2001a).
[127] OHM (2001a, 2001b, 2002a, 2002b, 2003).
[128] OHM (2002c).
[129] OHM (2000: 6).
[130] OHM (2002b).
[131] OHM (2004a: 1).
[132] Postgraduate Medical Education and Training Group (2006).
[133] Postgraduate Medical Education and Training Group (2006: 22).
[134] Comptroller and Auditor General (2007).
[135] Comptroller and Auditor General (2007: 47).
[136] Comptroller and Auditor General (2007: 47).
[137] HSE (2005).
[138] HSE (2008b).
[139] HSE (2008b: 42).
[140] HSE (2008b).
[141] HSE (2008d).

142 HSE (2008f).
143 HSE (2008e).
144 HSE (2008f).
145 HSE (2008e).
146 HSE (2009a).
147 HSE (2008d).

Chapter 7 – Governance and Clinical Directorates in Ireland

148 HSE (2009a).
149 HSE (2008d).
150 HSE (2009b).
151 HSE (2009b).
152 Mountford and Webb (2009).
153 Ministerial Task Group on Clinical Leadership (2009: 1).
154 Ministerial Task Group on Clinical Leadership (2009: 1).
155 Madden (2008).
156 Victorian Quality Council (2005: 2).
157 Donabedian (2003).
158 Donabedian (2003).
159 Mountford and Webb (2009).
160 NHS (2006).
161 HSE (2009b).
162 Huston (2009).
163 Huston (2009).
164 HSE (2009b).
165 Government of Ireland (2006).

Chapter 8 – Nursing and Midwifery and Clinical Directorates

166 HSE (2009a).
167 HSE (2009b).
168 CSO (2009).
169 CSO (2009).
170 HSE (2009a).
171 Scott et al. (2006).
172 Commission on Nursing (1998: 8.58).
173 National Council (2001a, 2001b, 2004a, 2004b, 2007a, 2007b, 2008a, 2008b).
174 The appendix contains a bibliography of all publications from the National Council.
175 National Council (2003).
176 National Council (2004c).

177 National Council (2005a).
178 National Council (2009).
179 Department of Health and Children (2001c).
180 Department of Health and Children (2001c).
181 Department of Health and Children (2003b).
182 See <http://www.skillproject.ie>.
183 O'Shea (2008a, 2008b).
184 Commission on Nursing (1998).
185 Commission on Nursing (1998).
186 Flynn (1998).
187 Department of Health and Children (2003c).
188 OHM (2002c).
189 HSE (2008e).
190 BAMM et al. (1993).
191 Buxton et al. (1989); Buxton et al. (1991); Packwood et al. (1991).
192 OPM (2003).
193 HSE (2009b).
194 NHS (2006).
195 OHM (2002c).
196 National Council (2005b).
197 Department of Health (UK) (2000).
198 An Bord Altranais and the National Council (2005).
199 An Bord Altranais (2007a, 2007b, 2007c, 2007d, 2007e).
200 O'Connell (2008).
201 National Council (2008a).
202 HSE (2008e).
203 National Council (2008c).
204 National Council (2008c).

Conclusion – A Challenge for all Professions
205 Department of Health and Children (2009c).

Appendix: Publications of the National Council for the Professional Development of Nursing and Midwifery

Clinical Nurse/Midwife Specialists Intermediate Pathway, Dublin: National Council (2001).

Framework for the Establishment of Advanced Nurse Practitioner and Advanced Midwife Practitioner Posts, Dublin: National Council (2001).

Criteria and Processes for the Allocation of Additional Funding for Continuing Education by the National Council, Dublin: National Council (2001).

Aid to Developing Job Descriptions/Profiles for Clinical Nurse/Midwife Specialists, Dublin: National Council (2001).

Guidelines on the Development of Courses Preparing Nurses and Midwives as Clinical Nurse/Midwife Specialists and Advanced Nurse/Midwife Practitioners, Dublin: National Council (2002).

Database of Third-Level Education Courses, Dublin: National Council (2002).

Agenda for the Future Professional Development of Nursing and Midwifery, Dublin: National Council (2003).

Guidelines for Portfolio Development for Nurses and Midwives, Dublin: National Council (2003).

Guidelines for Health Service Providers for the Selection of Nurses and Midwives who might Apply for Financial Support in Seeking Opportunities to Pursue Further Education, Dublin: National Council (2003).

Framework for the Establishment of Clinical Nurse/Midwife Specialist Posts Intermediate Pathway (Second Edition), Dublin: National Council (2004).

Framework for the Establishment of Advanced Nurse Practitioner and Advanced Midwife Practitioner Posts (Second Edition), Dublin: National Council (2004).

An Evaluation of the Effectiveness of the Role of the Clinical Nurse/Midwife Specialist, Dublin: National Council (2004).

Appendix

Report on the Continuing Professional Development of Staff Nurses and Midwives, Dublin: National Council (2004).

A Preliminary Evaluation of the Role of the Advanced Nurse Practitioner, Dublin: National Council (2005).

Service Needs Analysis for Clinical Nurse/Midwife Specialists and Advanced Nurse/Midwife Practitioners, Dublin: National Council (2005).

Agenda for the Future Professional Development of Public Health Nursing, Dublin: National Council (2005).

Clinical Nurse Specialist and Advanced Nurse Practitioner Roles in Emergency Departments: Position Paper, Dublin: National Council (2005).

A Study to Identify Research Priorities for Nursing and Midwifery in Ireland, Dublin: National Council (2005).

An Evaluation of the Extent and Nature of Nurse-Led/Midwife-Led Services in Ireland, Dublin: National Council (2005).

The Development of Joint Appointments: A Framework for Irish Nursing and Midwifery, Dublin: National Council (2005).

Review of Nurses and Midwives in the Prescribing and Administration of Medicinal Products (full and summary report), Dublin: National Council, with An Bord Altranais (2005).

Review of Achievements 2001 to 2006, Dublin: National Council (2006).

Clinical Nurse Specialist and Advanced Nurse Practitioner Roles in Intellectual Disability Nursing: Position Paper 2, Dublin: National Council (2006).

Report on the Baseline Survey of Research Activity in Irish Nursing and Midwifery, Dublin: National Council (2006).

Guidelines for Portfolio Development for Nurses and Midwives (Second Edition), Dublin: National Council (2006).

Measurement of Nursing and Midwifery Interventions: Guidance and Resource Pack, Dublin: National Council (2006).

Improving the Patient Journey: Understanding Integrated Care Pathways, Dublin: National Council (2006).

All-Ireland Practice and Quality Development Database Guide: A Guide to Sharing Practice and Quality Developments with Other Colleagues, Dublin: National Council (2006).

Framework for the Establishment of Clinical Nurse Specialist and Clinical Midwife Specialist Posts (Third Edition), Dublin: National Council (2007).

Appendix

Framework for the Establishment of Advanced Nurse Practitioner and Advanced Midwife Practitioner Posts (Third Edition), Dublin: National Council (2007).

Clinical Nurse Specialist and Advanced Nurse Practitioner Roles in Older Persons Nursing: Position Paper 3, Dublin: National Council (2007).

Criteria and Processes for the Allocation of Additional Funding for Continuing Education by the National Council (Second Edition), Dublin: National Council (2007).

The Introduction of Nurse and Midwife Prescribing in Ireland: An Overview, Dublin: National Council, with the HSE, the Department of Health and Children and An Bord Altranais (2007).

A Framework for the Establishment of Advanced Nurse Practitioner and Advanced Midwife Practitioner Posts (Fourth Edition), Dublin: National Council (2008).

Accreditation of Advanced Nurse Practitioners and Advanced Midwife Practitioners (Fourth Edition), Dublin: National Council (2008).

Profiles of Advanced Nurse/Midwife Practitioners and Clinical Nurse/Midwife Specialists in Ireland, Dublin: National Council (2008).

Annual Report and Accounts 2007, Dublin: National Council (2008).

Enhanced Nursing Practice in Emergency Departments: Position Paper 4, Dublin: National Council (2008).

Clinical Supervision: A Structured Approach to Best Practice, Dublin: National Council (2008).

Enhanced Midwifery Practice: Position Paper 5, Dublin: National Council (2008).

Report on the Role of the Nurse or Midwife in Medical-Led Clinical Research, Dublin: National Council (2008).

Profile of Clinical Nurse/Midwife Specialists and Advanced Nurse/Midwife Practitioners in Ireland, Dublin: National Council (2008).

Clinical Nurse/Midwife Specialist Role Resource Pack (Second Edition), Dublin: National Council with NMPDU, HSE (South) (2008).

Final Report of the Implementation of the Review of Nurses and Midwifes in Prescribing and Administration of Medicinal Products, Dublin: National Council, with An Bord Altranais (2008).

Framework for the Establishment of Clinical Nurse/Midwife Specialist Posts (Fourth Edition), Dublin: National Council (2008).

Appendix

Clinical Nurse/Midwife Specialists Resource Pack (Second Edition), Dublin and Kilkenny: National Council and Health Service Executive South (2008).

Evaluation of CNS/CMS and ANP/AMP in Ireland, work in progress – interim report due end of 2009, final report due in 2010, Dublin: National Council (2009).

Guidance on the Adaptation of Clinical Practice Guidelines: Getting Evidence into Practice, Dublin: National Council (2009).

Annual Report and Accounts 2008, Dublin: National Council (2009).

Review of Achievements 1999 to 2009, Ten Years, Dublin: National Council (2009).

Service Needs Analysis: Informing Business and Service Plans, Dublin: National Council (2009).

A Guide to the NCNM Online Research Database, Dublin: National Council (2009).

Guidelines for Portfolio Development for Nurses and Midwives (Third Edition), Dublin: National Council (2009).

Annual Reports of the National Council, 2000–2001, 2002, 2003, 2004, 2005, 2006, 2007, 2008.

National Council Newsletter/NCNM Quarterly Review, published quarterly, issues 1–28 (2001–2007).

NCNM Review, issues 29–32 (2008–2009).

REFERENCES

An Bord Altranais (2000a), *Scope of Nursing and Midwifery Practice Framework*, Dublin: An Bord Altranais.

An Bord Altranais (2000b), *Review of Scope of Practice for Nursing and Midwifery, Final Report*, Dublin: An Bord Altranais.

An Bord Altranais (2000c), *Code of Professional Conduct for Each Nurse and Midwife*, Dublin: An Bord Altranais.

An Bord Altranais (2007a), *Nurses Rules, 2007*, Dublin: An Bord Altranais.

An Bord Altranais (2007b), *Requirements and Standards for Education Programmes for Nurses and Midwives with Prescriptive Authority*, Dublin: An Bord Altranais.

An Bord Altranais (2007c), *Practice Standards for Nurses and Midwives with Prescriptive Authority*, Dublin: An Bord Altranais.

An Bord Altranais (2007d), *Decision-Making Framework for Nurses and Midwives with Prescriptive Authority*, Dublin: An Bord Altranais.

An Bord Altranais (2007e), *Collaborative Practice Agreement for Nurses and Midwives with Prescriptive Authority*, Dublin: An Bord Altranais.

An Bord Altranais and the National Council (National Council for the Professional Development of Nursing and Midwifery) (2005), *Review of Nurses and Midwives in the Prescribing and Administration of Medicinal Products – Final Report*, Dublin: An Bord Altranais and the National Council.

An Bord Altranais and the National Council (National Council for the Professional Development of Nursing and Midwifery) (2008), *Final Report of the Implementation of the Review of Nurses and Midwives in the Prescribing and Administration of Medicinal Products*, Dublin: An Bord Altranais and the National Council.

Baker, G.R. and Pink, G.H. (1995), 'A Balanced Scorecard for Canadian Hospitals', *Healthcare Management Forum*, 8(4): 7–21.

BAMM (British Association of Medical Managers), British Medical Association, Institute of Health Services, Royal College of Nursing (1993), *Managing Clinical Services: A Consensus Statement of Principles for Effective Clinical Management*, London: Institute of Health Services Management.

References

Barr, H. (2003), *Interprofessional Education: Today, Yesterday and Tomorrow – A Review*, commissioned by the Learning and Teaching Support Network for Health Sciences and Practice (LTSN) for the UK Centre for the Advancement of Interprofessional Education (CAIPE), <http://tinyurl.com/m28vnn>.

Barrington, R. (2000), *Health, Medicine and Politics in Ireland, 1900–1970*, Dublin: Institute of Public Administration.

Benner, P. (1984), *From Novice to Expert: Excellence and Power in Clinical Nursing Practice*, Menlo Park, CA: Addison-Wesley Publishing Company.

Benner, P., Hooper-Kyriakidis, P. and Stannard, D. (1999), *Clinical Wisdom and Interventions in Critical Care: A Thinking-in-Action Approach*, Philadelphia, PA: Saunders.

Beveridge, W. (1942), *Social Insurance and Allied Services*, London: Her Majesty's Stationery Office.

Braithwaite J. (2006), 'An Empirical Assessment of Social Structural and Cultural Change in Clinical Directorates', *Health Care Analysis*, 14(4): 185–193.

Braithwaite, J., Vining, R.F. and Lazarus, L. (1994), 'The Boundaryless Hospital', *Australian and New Zealand Journal of Medicine*, 24(5): 565–571.

Braithwaite, J. and Westbrook, M. (2005), 'Rethinking Clinical Organisational Structures: An Attitude Survey of Doctors, Nurses and Allied Health Staff in Clinical Directorates', *Journal of Health Services Research & Policy*, 10(1): 10–17.

Brennan Report (2003), see Commission on Financial Management and Control Systems in the Health Service.

Buttimer Report (2006), see Postgraduate Medical Education and Training Group.

Buxton, M., Packwood, T. and Keen, J. (1989), *Management: Process and Progress*, Uxbridge: Brunel University.

Buxton, M., Packwood, T. and Keen, J. (1991), *Final Report of the Brunel University Evaluation*, Uxbridge: Brunel University.

Callanan, I., McDermott, R. and Buttimer, A. (2002), 'Involving Irish Clinicians in Hospital Management Roles: Barriers to Successful Integration', *Clinicians in Management*, 11(1):37–46.

Capewell, S. (1992), 'Clinical Directorates: A Panacea For Clinicians Involved in Management?', *Health Bulletin*, 5(6): 441–447.

References

Central Statistics Office (CSO) (2009), *Women and Men in Ireland 2008*, Dublin: The Stationery Office.

Chantler, C. (1994), 'How to Treat Doctors: The Role of Clinicians in Management', *Speaking Up: Policy and Change in the NHS*, No. 3 (December), National Association of Health Authorities and Trusts (UK).

Commission on Financial Management and Control Systems in the Health Service (2003), *Report of the Commission on Financial Management and Control Systems in the Health Service* (the *Brennan Report*), Dublin: The Stationery Office.

Commission on Health Funding (1989), *Report of the Commission on Health Funding*, Dublin: The Stationery Office.

Commission on Nursing (1997), *Commission on Nursing Interim Report*, Dublin: The Stationery Office.

Commission on Nursing (1998), *Report of the Commission on Nursing: A Blueprint for the Future*, Dublin: The Stationery Office.

Comptroller and Auditor General (2007), *Comptroller and Auditor General Special Report: Medical Consultants' Contract*, Dublin: The Stationery Office.

Culliton, G. (2009), 'Clinical Directors Appointed', *Irish Medical Times*, 30 January 2009.

Dearden, W. (1990), *Resource Management and the Shape of the Organisation*, Bristol: NHS Training Authority.

Dedman, G.E. (2008), 'The Dimensions of Efficiency and Effectiveness of Clinical Directors in Western Australia's Public Teaching Hospitals', DBA thesis, <espace.library.curtin.edu.au/dtl_publish/39/115896.html>.

Department of Health (1947), *Outline of Proposals for the Improvement of the Health Services* (white paper), Dublin: Department of Health.

Department of Health (1971), *S.I. No. 187/1971: St James's Hospital Board (Establishment) Order, 1971*, Dublin: The Stationery Office.

Department of Health (1984), *S.I. No. 211/1984: St James's Hospital Board (Establishment) Order, 1971 (Amendment) Order, 1984*, Dublin: The Stationery Office.

Department of Health (1986), *Health: The Wider Dimensions (A Consultative Statement on Policy)*, Dublin: Department of Health and Children.

Department of Health (1994), *Shaping a Healthier Future: A Strategy for Effective Healthcare in the 1990s*, Dublin: Department of Health and Children.

References

Department of Health and Children (1996), *A Management Development Strategy for the Health and Personal Social Services in Ireland*, Dublin: Department of Health and Children.

Department of Health and Children (2001a), *Quality and Fairness: A Health System for You*, Dublin: Department of Health and Children.

Department of Health and Children (2001b), *Primary Care: A New Direction*, Dublin: Department of Health and Children.

Department of Health and Children (2001c), *Effective Utilisation of Professional Skills of Nurses and Midwives*, Dublin: Department of Health and Children.

Department of Health and Children (2002), *Action Plan for People Management*, Dublin: Department of Health and Children.

Department of Health and Children (2003a), *The Health Service Reform Programme*, Dublin: Department of Health and Children.

Department of Health and Children (2003b), *Evaluation of the Irish Pilot Programme for the Education of the Health Care Assistants*, Dublin: Department of Health and Children.

Department of Health and Children (2003c), *Nurses' and Midwives' Understanding and Experiences of Empowerment in Ireland*, Dublin: Department of Health and Children, Nursing Policy Division.

Department of Health and Children (2004), *Health Information: A National Strategy*, Dublin: Department of Health and Children.

Department of Health and Children (2008), *Statement of Strategy: 2008–2010*, Dublin: Department of Health and Children.

Department of Health and Children (2009a), 'Statement by the Minister for Health and Children Following Supplementary Budget', press release, 7 April 2009, <http://www.dohc.ie/press/releases/2009/20090407.html>.

Department of Health and Children (2009b), 'Mary Harney TD, Minister for Health and Children, Announces the Establishment of an Expert Group on Resource Allocation and Financing the Health Sector', press release, 1 April 2009, <http://www.dohc.ie/press/releases/2009/20090401.html>.

Department of Health and Children (2009c), 'Address at the University of Limerick by the Minister for Health and Children, Mary Harney TD', 22 January 2009, <http://www.dohc.ie/press/speeches/2009/20090122.html>.

Department of Health (UK) (1989), *Working for Patients*, London: Her Majesty's Stationery Office.

Department of Health (UK) (1998), *A First Class Service: Quality in the New NHS*, London: Her Majesty's Stationery Office.

Department of Health (UK) (2000), *The NHS Plan: A Plan for Investment, A Plan for Reform*, London: Her Majesty's Stationery Office.

Department of Health (UK) (2008), *High Quality Care: NHS Next Stage Review Final Report*, London: Her Majesty's Stationery Office.

Department of Social Welfare (1949), *Social Security* (white paper), Dublin: Department of Social Welfare.

DHSS (Department of Health and Social Security) (UK) (1986), *Health Services Management: Resource Management*, London: Department of Health and Social Security.

Disken, S., Dixon, M., Halpern, S. and Shocket, G. (1990), *Models of Clinical Management*, London: Institute of Health Services Management.

Donabedian, A. (2003), *An Introduction to Quality Assurance in Health Care*, Oxford: Oxford University Press.

Donaldson, L. and Muir Gray, J.A. (1998), 'Clinical Governance: A Quality Duty for Health Organisations', *Quality in Health Care*, 7 (supplement): S37–S44.

Donnellan, E. (2009), 'HSE to Divide Operations into Four Regions Across State', *Irish Times*, 8 May 2009.

Drucker, P. (1977), *People and Performance: The Best of Peter Drucker on Management*, London: Heinemann.

Drumm, B. (2008), 'HSE Reforms Aim to Deliver First Class Integrated Care to All', *Irish Times*, 10 July 2008.

Dyson, R. (1984), 'Griffiths Inquiry: A Personal Perspective', *British Medical Journal*, 288(6412): 255–257.

Edmondstone, J. and Chisnell, C. (1992), 'New Roles for Old', *Health Manpower Management*, 18(14): 34–35.

ECRI Institute (Emergency Care Research Institute), <http://www.ecri.org>.

FÁS (2005), *Health Care Skills Monitoring Report*, Dublin: FÁS.

Field, M.J. and Lohr, K.N. (1990), *Clinical Practice Guidelines: Directions for a New Program*, Washington DC: National Academy Press.

Fitzgerald, L. (1991), 'Made to Measure', *Health Services Journal*, 31 October 1991: 24–25.

Fitzgerald, L. (1992), 'Clinicians into Management: On the Change Agenda', *Health Services Management Research*, 5(2): 137–146.

References

Fitzgerald, P. (1968), *Report of the Consultative Council on the General Hospital Services*, Dublin: The Stationery Office.

Fleming, M. (2007), 'Clinicians in Management', *On Explication*, <http://tinyurl.com/mffdtf>.

Flynn, M. (1998), *Management in the Health Services: The Role of the Nurse – A Report Prepared for the Commission on Nursing*, Dublin: The Stationery Office.

Garelick, A. and Fagin, L. (2005), 'The Doctor–Manager Relationship', *Advances in Psychiatric Treatment*, 11(4): 241–250.

Goodwin, A. (1996), 'The Clinical-Manager Model in the NHS: Conflicting Social Defence Systems?', *International Journal of Psychoanalytic Psychotherapy*, 10(2): 125–133.

Gorman, L. (1987), 'Corporate Culture – Why Managers Should be Interested', *Leadership & Organisation Development Journal*, 8(5): 3–9.

Government of Ireland (1961), *Health (Corporate Bodies) Act, 1961*, Dublin: The Stationery Office.

Government of Ireland (1970), *Health Act, 1970*, Dublin: The Stationery Office.

Government of Ireland (2004), *Health Act, 2004*, Dublin: The Stationery Office.

Government of Ireland (2006), *A Vision for Change: Report of the Expert Group on Mental Health Policy*, Dublin: The Stationery Office.

Griffiths, R. (1983), *NHS Management Inquiry* (the *Griffiths Report*), London: Department of Health and Social Security.

Gupta, R.C. (2005), 'Review Use of Managers: In My View', *Hospital Doctor*, 12, 12 May 2005.

Gupta, R.C., Viadya, A. and Campbell, R. (2008), 'Analysing the Clinical Directorate System', *British Journal of Healthcare Management*, 14(9): 382–389.

Ham, C. and Hunter, D. (1988), 'Managing Clinical Activity in the NHS', Briefing Paper 8, London: King's Fund Institute.

Hanly Report (2003), see National Task Force on Medical Staffing.

Harding Clarke, M. (2006), *The Lourdes Hospital Inquiry: An Inquiry into Peripartum Hysterectomy at Our Lady of Lourdes Hospital, Drogheda*, Dublin: Department of Health and Children.

Harvey, B. (2007), *Evolution of Health Services and Health Policy in Ireland*, Dublin: Combat Poverty Agency.

Her Majesty's Government (UK) (1990), *National Health Service and Community Care Act, 1990*, London: Her Majesty's Stationery Office.

Hewitt-Taylor, J. (2003), 'National Recommendations and Guidelines', *Journal of Nursing Management*, 11(3): 158–163.

Hickey, K.J. (1990), *Community Medicine and Public Health: The Future Report of a Working Party Appointed by the Minister for Health*, Dublin: Department of Health and Children.

HIQA (Health Information and Quality Authority) (2008a), *Health Information and Quality Authority: Corporate Plan 2008–2010*, Dublin: HIQA.

HIQA (Health Information and Quality Authority) (2008b), *Health Information and Quality Authority: Business Plan 2008*, Dublin: HIQA.

Hopkins, A. (ed.) (1993), *The Role of Hospital Consultants in Clinical Directorates* (the *Synchromesh Report*), London: Royal College of Physicians.

HSE (Health Service Executive) (2005), *National Service Plan 2006*, Dublin: HSE.

HSE (Health Service Executive) (2006), *Transformation Programme 2007–2010*, Dublin: HSE.

HSE (Health Service Executive) (2008a), 'About the HSE', *Health Service Executive*, <http://www.hse.ie/eng/About_the_HSE/>.

HSE (Health Service Executive) (2008b), *Corporate Plan 2008–2011*, Dublin: HSE.

HSE (Health Service Executive) (2008c), *Transformation Programme Staff Briefing July 2008: National Integration – Local Responsibility*, HSE, <http://tinyurl.com/kmscxo>.

HSE (Health Service Executive) (2008d), *Clinical Directorates: The Way Forward, Briefing on Appointment of Clinical Directors throughout the Health Service, August 2008*, HMI, <http://tinyurl.com/d5wgzv>.

HSE (Health Service Executive) (2008e), *Proposed Terms and Conditions for a Contract of Employment for Consultants Employed in the Public Health Service*, Dublin: HSE.

HSE (Health Service Executive) (2008f), 'New Consultant Contract and Clinical Directorates Are a Major Step Forward', press release, 29 August 2008, <http://tinyurl.com/ofaz28>.

HSE (Health Service Executive) (2009a), *Clinical Directorates: Principles and Framework*, Dublin: HSE.

HSE (Health Service Executive) (2009b), *Achieving Excellence in Clinical Governance: A Distributed Clinical Leadership Model for the HSE – Ensuring the Health and Personal Social Care System Is In Good Hands*, Dublin: HSE.

HSE (Health Service Executive) (2009c), *Job Description for Regional Operations Director in the Health Service Executive*, Dublin: HSE.

HSE (Health Service Executive) (2009d), 'Clinicians in Management Breaking New Ground', *Health Matters*, Spring 2009 5(1):1.

HSE (Health Service Executive) (2009e), *Integrated Services Programme: Stage 1 Working Paper – Quality and Clinical Care Directorate*, Dublin: HSE.

Huston, M. (2009), 'New Chief with Big Challenges', *Irish Times Healthplus*, 7 April 2009.

Iles, V. and Sutherland, K. (2001), *Managing Change in the NHS – Organisational Change: A Review for Healthcare Managers, Professionals and Researchers*, London: NHS Service Delivery and Organisation (SDO) National R&D Programme.

Jones, C.S. and Dewing, I.P. (1997), 'The Attitudes of NHS Clinicians and Medical Managers Towards Changes in Accounting Controls', *Financial Accountability and Management*, 13(3): 261–280.

Kanter, R. (1993), *The Change Masters*, London: Allen and Unwin.

Keeley, P.W. (2003), 'Clinical Guidelines', *Palliative Medicine*, 17(4): 368–374.

Kennedy, D. (1991), *Reports* (three) *of the Dublin Hospitals Initiative Group 1990–1991*, Dublin: The Stationery Office.

Kennedy, I. (2001), *Learning from Bristol: The Report of the Public Inquiry into Children's Heart Surgery at the Bristol Royal Infirmary*, London: Her Majesty's Stationery Office.

Kitson, A. (1999), 'The Essence of Nursing', *Nursing Standard*, 13(23): 42–46.

Kowalczyk, R. (2002), 'The Effect of New Public Management on Intensive Care Unit Staff', *International Journal of Public Sector Management*, 15(2): 118–128.

Lansky, D. (1998), 'Perspective: Measuring What Matters to the Public', *Health Affairs*, 17(4): 40–41.

Llewellyn, S. (2001), '"Two-Way Windows": Clinicians as Medical Managers', *Organization Studies*, 22(4): 593–623.

MacLellan, K. (2007), 'Expanding Practice: Developments in Nursing and Career Pathways', *Nursing Management* (Harrow), 14(3): 28–34.

Madden, D. (2008), *Building a Culture of Patient Safety: The Report of the Commission on Patient Safety and Quality Assurance*, Dublin: Department of Health and Children.

Maddern, J., Courtney, M., Montgomery, J. and Nash, R. (2006), 'Strategy and Organisational Design in Health Care', in M.G. Harris (ed.), *Managing Health Services: Concepts and Practice* (Second Edition), Sydney: MacLennan and Petty.

Maxwell, R.J. (1992), 'Keynote Speech: On Hinges and Bridges', London: Institute of Health Services Management.

Maxwell, R.J. (1993), 'The Future of Clinical Directorates', in A. Hopkins (ed.), *The Role of Hospital Consultants in Clinical Directorates*, London: Royal College of Physicians.

McDermott, R., Callanan, I. and Buttimer, A. (2002), 'Involving Irish Clinicians in Hospital Management Roles: Towards a Functional Integration Model', *Clinicians in Management*, 11(1): 37–46.

McSherry, R. and Taylor, S. (2003), 'Developing Best Practice', in S. Pickering and J. Thompson (eds.), *Clinical Governance and Best Value: Meeting the Modernisation Agenda*, Edinburgh: Churchill Livingstone.

Ministerial Task Group on Clinical Leadership (2009), *In Good Hands: Transforming Clinical Governance in New Zealand*, February 2009, <http://www.nzihm.org.nz/documents/InGoodHandsReport.pdf>.

Mintzberg, H. (1981), 'Organisation Design: Fashion or Fit?', *Harvard Business Review*, 59(1): 103–116.

Mountford, J. and Webb, C. (2009), 'When Clinicians Lead', *The McKinsey Quarterly*, February 2009, <http://www.mckinseyquarterly.com/When_clinicians_lead_2293>.

Mui, L. (1997), 'Developing Medical Directors in Clinical Directorates', M.Phil. thesis, <http://groups.csail.mit.edu/medg/people/lmui/MedicalDirectors/>.

National Council (National Council for the Professional Development of Nursing and Midwifery) (2001a), *Clinical Nurse/Midwife Specialists Intermediate Pathway*, Dublin: National Council.

National Council (National Council for the Professional Development of Nursing and Midwifery) (2001b), *Framework for the Establishment of Advanced Nurse Practitioner and Advanced Midwife Practitioner Posts*, Dublin: National Council.

National Council (National Council for the Professional Development of Nursing and Midwifery) (2003), *Agenda for the Future Professional Development of Nursing and Midwifery*, Dublin: National Council.

National Council (National Council for the Professional Development of Nursing and Midwifery) (2004a), *Framework for the Establishment of Clinical Nurse/Midwife Specialist Posts Intermediate Pathway* (Second Edition), Dublin: National Council.

National Council (National Council for the Professional Development of Nursing and Midwifery) (2004b), *Framework for the Establishment of Advanced Nurse Practitioner and Advanced Midwife Practitioner Posts* (Second Edition), Dublin: National Council.

National Council (National Council for the Professional Development of Nursing and Midwifery) (2004c), *An Evaluation of the Effectiveness of the Role of the Clinical Nurse/Midwife Specialist*, Dublin: National Council.

National Council (National Council for the Professional Development of Nursing and Midwifery) (2005a), *A Preliminary Evaluation of the Role of the Advanced Nurse Practitioner*, Dublin: National Council.

National Council (National Council for the Professional Development of Nursing and Midwifery) (2005b), *Service Needs Analysis for Clinical Nurse/Midwife Specialists and Advanced Nurse/Midwife Practitioners*, Dublin: National Council.

National Council (National Council for the Professional Development of Nursing and Midwifery) (2006), *Improving the Patient Journey: Understanding Integrated Care Pathways*, Dublin: National Council.

National Council (National Council for the Professional Development of Nursing and Midwifery) (2007a), *Framework for the Establishment of Clinical Nurse Specialist and Clinical Midwife Specialist Posts* (Third Edition), Dublin: National Council.

National Council (National Council for the Professional Development of Nursing and Midwifery) (2007b), *Framework for the Establishment of Advanced Nurse Practitioner and Advanced Midwife Practitioner Posts* (Third Edition), Dublin: National Council.

National Council (National Council for the Professional Development of Nursing and Midwifery) (2008a), *A Framework for the Establishment of Advanced Nurse Practitioner and Advanced Midwife Practitioner Posts* (Fourth Edition), Dublin: National Council.

National Council (National Council for the Professional Development of Nursing and Midwifery) (2008b), *Accreditation of Advanced Nurse*

Practitioners and Advanced Midwife Practitioners (Fourth Edition), Dublin: National Council.

National Council (National Council for the Professional Development of Nursing and Midwifery) (2009), *Evaluation of CNS/CMS and ANP/AMP in Ireland*, work in progress – interim report due end of 2009, final report due in 2010, Dublin: National Council.

National Council (National Council for the Professional Development of Nursing and Midwifery) and HSE (Health Service Executive) South, (2008), *Clinical Nurse/Midwife Specialists Resource Pack* (Second Edition), Dublin and Kilkenny: National Council and Health Service Executive South.

National Task Force on Medical Staffing (2003), *Report of the National Task Force on Medical Staffing* (the *Hanly Report*), Dublin: Department of Health and Children.

New Zealand Guidelines Group (NZGG) (2001), *Handbook for the Preparation of Explicit Evidence-Based Clinical Practice Guidelines*, Wellington: New Zealand Guidelines Group.

NHS Institute for Innovation and Improvement (2006), *The NHS Leadership Qualities Framework*, <http://www.NHSLeadershipQualities.nhs.uk>.

NICE (National Institute for Health and Clinical Excellence) (2007), 'About Clinical Guidelines', *National Institute for Health and Clinical Excellence*, <http://www.nice.org.uk/guidance/index.jsp>.

O'Connell, F. (2008), 'Sharing the Care of COPD', *Irish Medical Times*, 40, 22 February 2008.

OHM (Office for Health Management) (2000), 'A Temperature Check – Clinicians in Management Initiative', *Office for Health Management Newsletter*, 5(October): 5–6.

OHM (Office for Health Management) (2001a), *Clinicians in Management Discussion Paper 1: Introduction and Case Studies*, Dublin: OHM.

OHM (Office for Health Management) (2001b), *Clinicians in Management Discussion Paper 2: A Framework for Discussion*, Dublin: OHM.

OHM (Office for Health Management) (2002a), *Clinicians in Management Discussion Paper 3: A Review of the Initiative and Pointers to the Way Forward*, Dublin: OHM.

OHM (Office for Health Management) (2002b), *Clinicians in Management Discussion Paper 4: A Review of Clinical Leadership*, Dublin: OHM.

OHM (Office for Health Management) (2002c), *Report on Nursing Management Competencies*, Dublin: OHM.

References

OHM (Office for Health Management) (2003), *Clinicians in Management Discussion Paper 5: Clinicians in Management at Work in Mayo General Hospital, Choices in CIM*, Dublin: OHM.

OHM (Office for Health Management) (2004a), 'Clinicians in Management and the Reform Agenda', *Office for Health Management Newsletter*, 1(February): 1–3.

OHM (Office for Health Management) (2004b), *Clinicians in Management: Charter of Rights and Responsibilities for Hospital Managers and Consultants*, Dublin: OHM.

OPM (Office for Public Management) (2003), *Learning from the NHS in Change: A Study on the Management of Major Structural Change in the NHS*, Dublin: OHM.

O'Shea, Y. (1992), 'Quality Assurance in Nursing in a General Hospital: The Experience of St James's Hospital, Dublin', B.A. (Health Admin.) dissertation, Institute of Public Administration (IPA)/National Council for Educational Awards (NCEA) (unpublished).

O'Shea, Y. (1995), 'Resource Management and the Clinical Directorate Model: Implications for St James's Hospital Dublin', M.Sc. Econ. dissertation, Trinity College Dublin (unpublished).

O'Shea, Y. (2008a), *Nursing and Midwifery in Ireland: A Strategy for Professional Development in a Changing Health Service*, Dublin: Blackhall Publishing.

O'Shea, Y. (2008b), 'Strengthening the Contribution of Nursing and Midwifery to Health and Healthcare in Ireland: A Strategy for Professional Development in a Changing Health Service', Ph.D. thesis, Trinity College Dublin (unpublished).

Packwood, M., Keen, J. and Buxton, M. (1991), *Hospitals in Transition: The Resource Management Experiment*, Milton Keynes: Open University Press.

Petasnick, W.D. (2007), 'Hospital–Physician Relationships: Imperative for Clinical Enterprise Collaboration', *Frontiers of Health Service Management*, 24(1): 3–10.

Postgraduate Medical Education and Training Group (2006), *Preparing Ireland's Doctors to Meet the Health Needs of the 21st Century: Report of the Postgraduate Medical Education and Training Group* (the *Buttimer Report*), Dublin: The Stationery Office.

Prospectus Strategy Consultants (2003), *Audit of Structures and Functions in the Health System, 2003* (the *Prospectus Report*), Dublin: The Stationery Office.

References

Public Services Organisation Review Group (1969), *Report of the Public Services Organisation Review Group, 1966–1969* (the *Devlin Report*), Dublin: The Stationery Office.

Rea, C. (1992), 'Gang Mentality', *Health Services Journal*, 102(5295): 31–32, 34.

Rea, C. (1995), 'Clinical Directorates', *British Journal of Health Care Management* 1(4): 213–214.

Rivett, G. (2009), *National Health Service History*, <http://www.nhshistory.net>.

Rosenberg, C. (1987), *The Care of Strangers: The Rise of America's Hospital System*, New York: Basic Books.

Royal College of Nursing (RCN) (1990), *Clinical Directorates and Nursing*, London: Royal College of Nursing.

St James's Hospital, Dublin (1990–2007), *Annual Reports*, Dublin: St James's Hospital.

St James's Hospital, Dublin (1992), *St James's Hospital Total Hospital Information Systems Strategic Plan*, Dublin: St James's Hospital.

St James's Hospital, Dublin (1996), *Tender for the Establishment and Provision of Cardiac Surgery Services at St James's Hospital*, Dublin: St James's Hospital.

Schein, E.A. (1985), *Organisation Culture and Leadership: A Dynamic View*, San Francisco, CA: Jossey-Bass.

Schidt, I., Andrews, S. and Turner, S. (1995), 'Bringing Clinicians into Management', *British Journal of Health Care Management*, 1(1): 24–26.

Scott, P.A., Hayes, E. and MacNeela, P. (2006), *An Exploration of the Core Nursing Elements of Care Provided by Registered General Nurses Within the Community Setting*, Dublin: Dublin City University.

Scottish Executive (2009), *Health and Social Care Data Directory*, <http://www.datadictionaryadmin.scot.nhs.uk/isddd/1888.html>.

Severs, M. and Bowers, H. (1993), 'Management of Nursing Services within Clinical Directorates' in A. Hopkins (ed.), *The Role of Hospital Consultants in Clinical Directorates*, London: Royal College of Physicians.

Shipman, D. (2007), 'The Solution to Hospital/Physician Relations is Management', *Practice Support*, <http://www.practicesupport.com/attitude.pdf>.

SKILL Project, <http://www.skillproject.ie>.

References

Smith, J. and Ham, C. (2000), 'An Evaluative Commentary on Health Services Management at Bristol: Setting Key Evidence in a Wider Normative Context' in I. Kennedy (chair) (2001), *Learning from Bristol: The Report of the Public Inquiry into Children's Heart Surgery at the Bristol Royal Infirmary*, London: Her Majesty's Stationery Office.

Spurgeon, P. (2001), 'Managing "Cultural" Differences in Health Services Involving Clinicians in Management: A Challenge of Perspective', *Health Care and Informatics Review Online*, 5(4), 1 August 2001.

Stepheny, S. (1993), 'Role of the Business Manager in Clinical Directorates', in A. Hopkins (ed.), *The Role of Hospital Consultants in Clinical Directorates*, London: Royal College of Physicians.

Thorne, M.L. (1997), 'Being a Clinical Director: First Among Equals or Just a Go-Between?', *Health Service Management Research*, 10(4): 205–215.

Turrill, T. (1990), *Resource Management: Changing the Culture*, Bristol: NHS Training Authority.

Victorian Quality Council (2005), *Developing the Clinical Leadership Role in Clinical Governance: A Guide for Clinicians and Health Services*, <http://tinyurl.com/nnub9a>, Melbourne: Metropolitan Health and Aged Care Services Division Victorian Government Department of Human Services.

Walker, D. (1993), 'Benefits of Clinical Directorates' in A. Hopkins (ed.), *The Role of Hospital Consultants in Clinical Directorates*, London: Royal College of Physicians.

White, T. (1993), *Management for Clinicians: A Dynamic View*, London: Edward Arnold Publishers.

Willcocks, S. (1994), 'Organizational Analysis: A Health Service Commentary', *Leadership & Organization Development Journal*, 15(1): 29–32.

Willcocks, S. (1997), 'Managerial Effectiveness in the NHS: A Possible Framework for Considering the Effectiveness of the Clinical Director', *Journal of Management in Medicine*, 11(3): 181–189.

WHO (World Health Organisation) (1981), *Global Strategy for Health for All by the Year 2000*, Geneva: WHO.

Zwarenstein, M., Atkins, J., Barr, H., Hammick, M., Koppel, I. and Reeves, S. (1999), 'A Systematic Review of Interprofessional Education', *Journal of Interprofessional Care*, 13(4): 417–424.

INDEX